VETA T. RICHARDSON
& *TAKE SIX*

Veta Richardson has counseled, coached, and advised me along the path that led to achievement of my dream of becoming a nonprofit chief executive officer. She is an extraordinary leader and an even more extraordinary career strategist and advisor. I'm confident that her new book, Take Six, will be an invaluable resource for individuals at any place along their leadership journey.

—ONA DOSUNMU,
NONPROFIT ASSOCIATION CEO

I call upon Veta for advice because her candor and unparalleled experiences guide me on my path of professional and personal growth. Being the "ride-or-die mentor" that she is, Veta helps me create those moments of looking in the mirror and being proud of who I am becoming.

—QUINCEY WILSON,
*GRADUATE STUDENT (LAW),
CLASS OF 2023*

Veta's kindness, experiences, inspiring personality, and unwavering confidence in her people have been a guide for me as her mentee for years—going back to her, a well of knowledge and encouragement, for many wildly meaningful and timely conversations. It is in those conversations where she reminds you of who you are, what you have already accomplished, and how you are on your way to accomplish so much more that gives you the resolve to keep going, to ask for more, to take the risk. She sees the best in you and pulls it out to push you forward.

—DANIELLE WHITE,
*SENIOR LEGAL COUNSEL TO GLOBAL
TECHNOLOGY COMPANY*

Veta is a trusted colleague and well-respected connector of people. She is a champion of the organizations she leads, tackling business challenges with confidence, compassion, and decisiveness.

—KENT K. MATSUMOTO,
*CORPORATE EXECUTIVE AND
PROFESSIONAL COLLEAGUE*

A few years back, life had brought me to China; I was appointed to a leadership position for which I had no prior training or guidance to call upon. When confiding in a friend about my challenges, she strongly recommended that I reach out to Veta. That was, by far, the greatest leadership training I have ever received. Veta's words still resonate with me. She wholeheartedly opened up her schedule for me, guided me through a series of questions, and allowed me to discover who I was and what kind of leader I would aspire to be. Through our conversations, I was enlightened on how to guide new members who entered our team and empower them to bring out the best in themselves. In a short timeframe, we flourished and succeeded, and I strongly believe that this was due to Veta helping me clarify and lay down the foundations of our core, soul, and purpose. I am forever grateful.

—EFTYCHIA GAVRIIL,
*EDUCATOR AND HEAD OF
MUSIC DEPARTMENT AT INTERNATIONAL
SCHOOL FOR CHILDREN*

TAKE SIX

TAKE STOCK

TAKE RISK

TAKE CREDIT

TAKE A HAND

TAKE A STAND

TAKE COMMAND

VETA T. RICHARDSON

TAKE
SIX

ESSENTIAL HABITS TO OWN YOUR DESTINY, OVERCOME CHALLENGES, AND UNLOCK OPPORTUNITIES

ForbesBooks

Published by ForbesBooks, Charleston, South Carolina.
Member of Advantage Media Group.

ForbesBooks is a registered trademark, and the ForbesBooks colophon is a trademark of Forbes Media, LLC.

Printed in the United States of America.

10 9 8 7 6 5 4 3 2 1

ISBN: 978-1-95086-355-6
LCCN: 2021907657

Cover and layout designed by David Taylor.

This custom publication is intended to provide accurate information and the opinions of the author in regard to the subject matter covered. It is sold with the understanding that the publisher, Advantage|ForbesBooks, is not engaged in rendering legal, financial, or professional services of any kind. If legal advice or other expert assistance is required, the reader is advised to seek the services of a competent professional.

 Advantage Media Group is proud to be a part of the Tree Neutral® program. Tree Neutral offsets the number of trees consumed in the production and printing of this book by taking proactive steps such as planting trees in direct proportion to the number of trees used to print books. To learn more about Tree Neutral, please visit **www.treeneutral.com.**

Since 1917, Forbes has remained steadfast in its mission to serve as the defining voice of entrepreneurial capitalism. ForbesBooks, launched in 2016 through a partnership with Advantage Media Group, furthers that aim by helping business and thought leaders bring their stories, passion, and knowledge to the forefront in custom books. Opinions expressed by ForbesBooks authors are their own. To be considered for publication, please visit **www.forbesbooks.com.**

To my sister, Vicki, whose intelligence, resilience, and curiosity never cease to inspire. You are living proof that a smart woman can excel at any pursuit she sets her mind to achieve and that the biggest risk is being too afraid to try. I love and admire you!

CONTENT

TAKE SIX

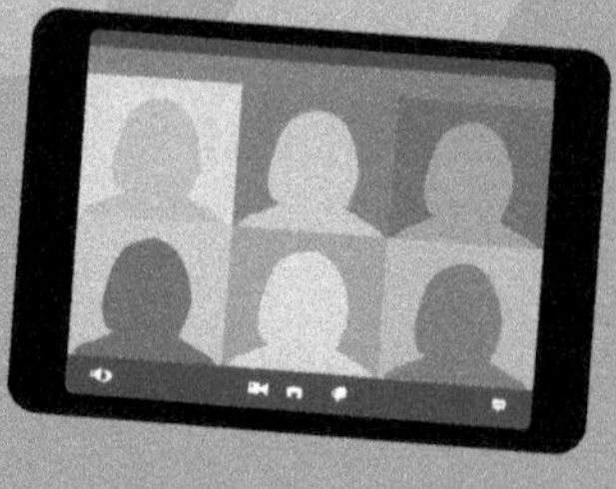

FOREWORD

BY DEBRA HILTON

One of the things I love about ghostwriting is the ability to delve into another person's hard-won experience, knowledge, and practical wisdom and be the channel through which their ideas are brought to the world in book form. Usually, I work behind the scenes, often with rigorous NDAs, so when Veta asked me to write her foreword, my first response was, "Do you think that's OK with the publisher?"

Veta's response was a question that came up many times as we worked on this book: "What would happen if you did write the foreword and made it about you, the ghostwriter?" Over the months we've worked together I've learned that when she makes me feel uncomfortable, she's usually on to something, so I sent her the first version of this foreword only to have it returned with the comment, "It's very well written, but what would happen (apart from you feeling uncomfortable) if you made it a bit more personal, answered some of my questions, and gave people an insight into the journey we've been on together over these past months?" And so I have followed her advice—because I have learned to trust her.

I have ghostwritten many nonfiction books at this time, including seven *New York Times* best sellers, and I love turning the expertise and personality of others into an enjoyable book. Books hold a special place in my life (and fill my home) because they let you learn from and converse with people from different times and places.

I write other people's stories rather than my own for three reasons: first, I like seeing things from inside another person's perspective; second, I have a high tolerance for living risk, but a great respect for unintended consequences of my stories and their potential impact on the innocent; and third, there are ideas, concepts, and stories that need to be told powerfully and persuasively so that the world will pay attention.

Let me explain each of those reasons a little more.

While I was still in high school, I determined what I wanted my life to look like and started to Take Stock so I could make that happen. My goal was to see different cultures and ways of life from the inside rather than as a tourist. I have had the immense privilege of living and working as a semi-insider for over twenty-five years in rural towns in Indonesia, Chad, and Mozambique through war and peace. Most of the time, that meant that I spent my waking hours speaking a foreign language because there were few anglophones outside our own family. That habit of developing a semi-insider perspective through listening, studying the subject, and learning to reflect another person's voice is an important quality for a ghostwriter (I would argue that if everyone practiced it a bit more often our world would be a better place) because you need to set aside your own preconceptions if you want to communicate the ideas with conviction.

My first book was about the political situation in one of our homes and its impact on our long-suffering neighbors. I realized that to publish it would jeopardize other people's lives and careers and, taken out of context, also damage the reputation of organizations that do valuable work. I'm happy to Take Risk on a personal level, but the potential cost of my self-indulgence was too high, and I know that "anonymity" only goes so far even if you clothe the truth in fiction. As I considered other book ideas from my own experience, I kept running up against the same concerns until a friend suggested that rather than piling up the pages that were destined to never be read, I turn my hand to ghostwriting—an area of writing that lets other people Take Risk of exposure and helps them Take Credit for their ideas as they gain a wider readership.

Have you ever heard someone speak powerfully then bought their book and been disappointed? I was still at university when I heard a man who survived the bombing at Pearl Harbor and then spent decades in Japan as a missionary tell the story of his life lessons on courage, forgiveness, and choice. Despite his raspy voice (legacy of Pearl Harbor) he was a spell-binding speaker, so I rushed out and bought his book. The stories were the same, but the impact and personality had vanished completely, because speeches aren't books and speakers aren't necessarily writers. I set it aside—just as many hastily produced business books are set aside.

As a ghostwriter, I work with some people who don't have time to write their own books, others who know they don't have the skills to write a book (even if they are proficient at writing), and still others who potentially could write their own book, but know that working alongside someone at the writing stage (rather than just the editing stage) will make their book more influential. As Veta said, working with me made her probe and think about the reasons behind her methods and recommendations in ways she hadn't previously done. She was grateful to Take a Hand in her first effort to produce a manuscript for publication, and I have also learned many valuable lessons from her material that I'll be applying as I move forward.

Writing a book is transformative in many ways. Sometimes you discover new things about your model as your manuscript grows—a book is like a child in this: it grows in surprising ways. Six Habits started life as Six Principles, but we quickly realized that understanding and believing they are true is not enough, nor is practicing them occasionally ... to be truly effective, these Six Habits need to be habitual behaviors that propel you from where you are to where (and who) you want to be. Veta and I talked on Zoom almost every week for six months as we worked on the various iterations of her book. It was an appointment I looked forward to each week. We both found it therapeutic as we lived through our shared but different experiences of the pandemic lockdown on different sides of the globe and focused on the overarching goal: to help people realize that they could take control of many aspects of their lives rather than just saying, "That's the way my life is and must be."

TESTED AND TRIED

It's easy to see how greatly people value Veta's contribution to their lives as well as her practiced approach to mentoring and providing honest feedback as you listen to her stories and speak to the people who have helped her and been helped by her. I honestly believe that when you adopt these six habits for yourself, you'll **stop** making excuses and blaming others for things that aren't the way you want them to be and **start** to see more and more things turning out the way you'd like them to be. In other words, you'll find yourself owning your destiny, overcoming challenges, unlocking opportunities, and building a better world for us all.

Actually, the existence of this book is a demonstration of the way Veta practices these habits herself. She asked, "How can I mentor more people with my finite time?" Then she committed to the risky business of putting her ideas out in the world in concrete form, willingly investing her time, energy, and attention into the effort, and preparing to risk any criticism and stand up for her ideas in order to help others reach their goals. Finally, she took command and ownership of every aspect of the book with her habitual courage, forthrightness, and grace.

TAKE ACTION

Don't just read this book.

No matter where you are in your career, take notes, make these habits part of your life plan, and set your sights on making an impact. If there is one big lesson I took away from *Take Six*, it is this: no matter who you are, there is always an opportunity to make a difference if you choose to do so—and it starts with you.

TAKE SIX

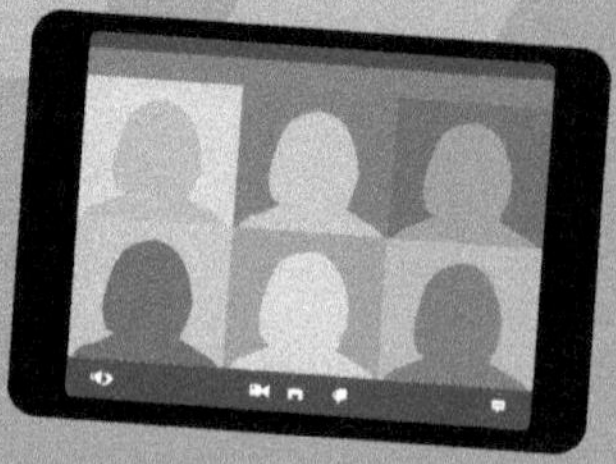

INTRODUCTION

If there's a book you want to read, but it hasn't
been written yet, then you must write it.

—TONI MORRISON

I was twenty-two years old and had just completed my second year of law school as I walked into the corporate headquarters of Sunoco on the first day of my summer internship. My heart was racing, my stomach filled with butterflies, and the sounds of my heels clicking against the polished floor of that palatial lobby made me feel even more self-conscious. This was my opportunity of a lifetime! I'd been dreaming of a day like this ever since I first declared my goal to pursue a career in corporate law—a dream that I first verbalized back in elementary school with my hair braided in two long pigtails.

As I gave my name to the receptionist, I felt a tinge of fear. Maybe it would not be on the list. Maybe she would say what I was thinking as I looked around the spacious reception area—that I did not belong. Instead, she smiled and asked me to take a seat on a leather sofa in one of several carefully staged seating areas while someone came to meet me. As I waited in the beautiful reception area for my escort to arrive and show me to the law department where I would spend the summer, I felt my self-confidence oozing away and my nerves and fear of failure overwhelming me with questions. "What am I doing here? What on earth makes me think I could work for the law department at a *Fortune* 500 company?"

Everything was so large. Shiny. Sophisticated. The lobby looked out onto the meticulously manicured lawn, flower gardens, outdoor sculptures, and pond with its spouting fountain. Everyone who strode through the lobby as I waited looked purposeful, polished, confident ... as the only African American in the summer program, I definitely stood out, no matter how much I wished to blend in with the others.

Each day throughout that summer, I went to work determined to dig in, work hard, tackle each assignment, meet the expectations of the assigning attorneys, and prove my worth to the company ... and to myself. Every night, I came home and cried because I felt like a fraud. I was desperately afraid of failure and worried that I could never measure up or fit in with their standards. Each night, my sister and mother reassured me that I was smart enough. That I could do it if I would just stick with it. Their reassurance helped me to press on and keep giving it everything I could. The work was so interesting, an absorbing mix of business and legal issues that totally aligned with my career goals, and I was totally hooked—but the gap between where I was and where I wanted to be seemed as wide as an ocean.

At the end of the summer, I received a shiny new leather briefcase as a parting gift, and when I went back to law school, I felt grateful for the whole summer experience. My end-of-program reviews were all positive. At some point during that summer, I went from scared and self-doubting to validated and capable. The experience also confirmed that my career goals weren't pipe dreams; I **could** succeed in corporate law, even though I had no idea how or when that might eventually happen for me. I even dreamed of (one day) working at Sunoco again. Then, a few weeks after returning for my third and final year of law school, the head of legal at Sunoco called and offered me a job starting after I graduated in the spring. I was so shocked that I asked him to repeat his offer in case I had misheard. Once I confirmed that he had truly offered me a full-time position, I accepted the offer immediately ... before he had time to change his mind!

I'll go into more detail about the importance of that internship later in the book, and especially the strategy I used to secure the internship at Sunoco that summer despite initial rejection. For the moment, I simply want to say that nothing about that internship was a given. It would never have happened if I hadn't taken stock of where I was and what I needed to reach my goal, and then been willing to take some big risks, refuse to take no for an answer, track my contributions, and ask for help along the way. As I look back, that summer forever changed my career trajectory for the better, introduced me to lifelong mentors and friends, taught several critical life lessons, and laid the groundwork for the woman I was to become.

HOW THIS BOOK CAN HELP YOU

There are many books that teach you how to get into the college of your choice, how the system works, and how to follow the path that others have laid out.

This book takes a different approach. My focus is on helping **you** define what success looks like and plot your own pathway from where you are to where you want to be based on your personal goals and hard work. It is a book that I would have liked to have had beside me as I planned my own career. In it, I outline the six key habits that I share with those I mentor and draw on my own years of experience, research findings about career development, discussions with senior management, and advice I received from the many people who generously gave me their time, energy, and advice as they mentored me and encouraged me to step up, own my strengths, and learn to lead while being my authentic self rather than trying to copy someone else.

One of the important realities I hope to convey is that nerves, confidence, growth, and competence can go hand in hand. That flutter of nerves and pounding of the heart when you meet a challenge head on isn't a sign that you're not ready for the challenge; it's a sign that you care about the outcome and that you're willing to learn and grow. Another key takeaway is that there is documented research into actions that give your career momentum and those that hold you back. This book draws on that research and provides practical ways to increase your momentum and reduce unnecessary friction.

I didn't know, when I walked into Sunoco for my first day as an unpaid intern and for the first time felt that I was completely out of my league, where that experience would lead me. Perhaps if I'd had these six habits spelled out in front of me that summer, I might still have felt the same insecurities and urgent desire to fit in, but I might also have realized that the young woman that I was then had a valuable contribution to make.

> **One of the important realities I hope to convey is that nerves, confidence, growth, and competence can go hand in hand.**

This book doesn't just tell my stories. You will also discover untold stories of everyday heroes whose hard work and dedication enabled them to create their own luck and turn challenges into growth and opportunity.

It is my hope that reading this book will give you the courage to step into who you are and cross any perceived barriers to achievement—barriers that previously seemed to limit your opportunities and restrict your horizons. My hope is that what I have to share will help you to create the life and career of your dreams, no matter what the world around you deems possible or makes you feel may be impossible.

WHY LISTEN TO ME?

There is a simple answer based on my personal achievements and a more nuanced answer based on the help that my advice has provided to hundreds of people over many years. As you read this book and discover how these six habits can help you own your destiny and vision for your future, overcome the challenges that you encounter, and unlock new opportunities for yourself, you'll be introduced to some of the people whom I have been privileged to mentor or be mentored by through the years. One thing that I hope will stand out is that, like me, these men and women did not have success handed to them on a platter. They earned their success through disciplined, consistent implementation of these practices, and they worked hard to shape their lives the way they wanted and own their destinies. As they followed these habits, they discovered ways of overcoming seemingly insurmountable obstacles, turning rejection into acceptance, and creating opportunity where none previously existed. No matter what goals and aspirations you have or how they shift, these habits will help you create your own "luck" as you move steadily forward.

Against the odds, I was able to complete my undergraduate degree in just three years, get into law school on my own merits, and receive an offer to start my professional career at Sunoco, then one of the largest corporations in the United States. When I left Sunoco to move to Washington, DC, and take the position of deputy general counsel with what is now ACC (then ACCA or American Corporate Counsel Association, now the global Association of Corporate

Counsel), I left a comfortable career path to pursue new challenges creating educational programs and services for the in-house counsel sector of the legal profession.

In 2001, after being at ACC almost four years, I was recruited by the Minority Corporate Counsel Association (MCCA) as executive director. MCCA's focus was specifically on developing opportunities for underrepresented groups in the legal profession (women, racial/ethnic minorities, people with disabilities, and LGBTQ+), and MCCA undertook substantial research to assess the situation and offer recommendations. During the ten years I worked there, I took the organization from insolvency (in my first month, we had to draw from a line of credit to meet payroll) to financial stability. Along the way, I became a thought leader in the field of diversity and inclusion and was called upon to advise three US presidential administrations (Clinton, Bush, Obama) and hundreds of global executives before being recruited to return to ACC in my current position as president and CEO.

None of this was handed to me on a platter. Along the way, I made choices and created connections that shaped my opportunities. I worked hard. And I learned how to stand up for myself, my beliefs, my values, my rights and those of others, and to insist we be treated with respect, and to see how much we are all shaped by the world around us.

My experience is primarily in the legal and business worlds, but the principles I'm sharing are widely applicable and useful for anyone who wants to branch out and create new opportunities. Not long ago, I was advising Nicole, a young woman who had recently completed her graduate studies and wanted to pursue a career in the fashion industry, focusing on the business aspects. Although my knowledge of fashion merchandising is very limited, the questions and principles I shared (especially with respect to taking stock) were useful for guiding her analysis of her professional situation and charting potential next steps for her job search.

WHY YOU SHOULD READ THIS BOOK

Biographies and personal growth books are powerful lenses through which you can gain perspective, especially when you are trying to forge your own path to success. It is an interesting paradox because we are all torn between the desire to fit in and the desire to be different, to express our unique personalities yet not be considered odd. I have never been able to hide my identity as a person of color, nor have I wanted to do so, because for me, it's a source of great strength. But I was tempted to try to fit in in other ways, even if that meant hiding what I really wanted or the things that were of interest to me. Maybe you have been trying to hide your uniqueness because the world values conformity. Possibly, you're feeling so overwhelmed by the challenges or disappointments you've experienced that you just want to walk away and hide. Perhaps you want to find a way to influence others and share your vision of hope. The secret is that most of the people you meet are like that too.

I believe that reading my story and discovering the habits that have brought me from where I started as an introverted teenager to the very visible, externally facing role that I fill today will help you make the critical decisions that will shape your life and widen your sphere of influence.

These six habits were my road map, even before I articulated them. They are the consistent actions that I have built into my schedule and behavior to embed as essential habits that have enabled me to

- pursue stretch opportunities and convey my ability to execute them;

- build a substantial network of connections across a variety of industries;

- offer advice and strategies to hundreds of people seeking to clarify and pursue their goals;

- reach out and give a helping hand to young professionals in need of mentoring as well as ask others to help me succeed;

- navigate organizations and lead teams through extreme financial challenges and business disruption;

- overcome biases, whether overt or covert, and earn the appreciation and respect of a global network of professionals; and, perhaps most importantly ...

- demonstrate the power of perseverance, diligence, and strategic pursuit of dreams as I encourage others to do the same.

In the following chapters, we will dive into each of the habits individually and explore the roles they play (both individually and as a group) in shaping your success, especially if you feel that you are facing exceptional challenges and that there are many barriers to your success.

These six essential habits are as follows:

1. Take Stock: Assess who you are, where you are, where you want to end up, and what gaps you need to fill to get there.

2. Take Risk: Increase your tolerance of risk and step out of your comfort zone while also exercising good judgment. Be willing to try something totally new, make mistakes and overcome them, or volunteer for a difficult project.

3. Take Credit: Learn to accept credit as your due for a job well done instead of immediately deflecting it to others and minimizing your role. Always acknowledge the contributions others made, but not at your own expense.

4. Take a Hand: Recognize that other people are both able and willing to help you move forward. Stick your neck out to ask for and accept help where you need it as well as lend a hand to boost someone else.

5. Take a Stand: Understand the value of your voice, know when to raise it to speak out against a wrong or violation of your values, and learn how to do so effectively, respectfully, and constructively.

6. Take Command: Lead with authority and confidence, and act decisively in the best interests of stakeholders without compromising your own authenticity and integrity. As a leader you should never defer to how the person who preceded you would do things if that is not congruent with your own style and conviction.

Perhaps you are already prepared to step up and become the leader you aspire to be, and you need some strategic advice. Maybe you know that your career has stalled, and you need some kind of boost or jump start to get things moving, but you don't know where to turn. You may even just be starting out and trying to determine in which direction you should take your professional aspirations. In any of these cases, right now is the perfect time to clarify your priorities and decide where you want to go and what you need to focus on in order to get there. As these principles become your habits, they will offer a road map to help you move forward more confidently.

In the next chapter, you'll learn more about who I am, the people and experiences that shaped my perspectives, and how these principles started to take root way before I had the clarity to put them together as *Take Six*. This will help you see how you can take these principles and adopt them as essential habits.

TAKE SIX

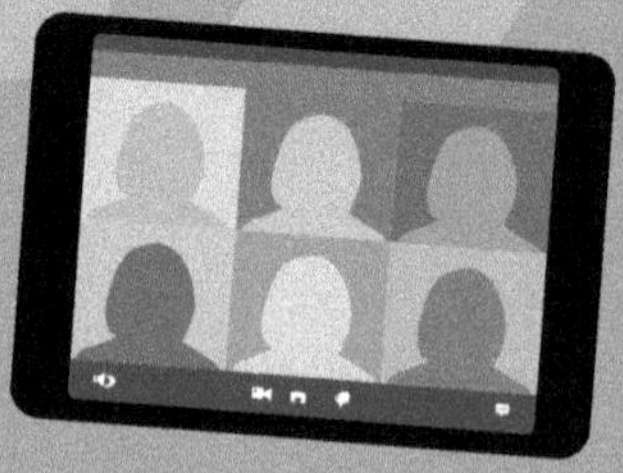

CHAPTER ONE

DISCOVERING THE SIX ESSENTIAL HABITS FOR SUCCESS

Don't follow the path. Go where there is no path and begin the trail. When you start a new trail equipped with courage, strength, and conviction, the only thing that can stop you is you!

—RUBY BRIDGES

I was eight years old when I realized that things would happen to me that didn't make sense to me or to anyone who loved me just because of the color of my skin. It stung me to the core, and it changed the way I perceived circumstances and people. I learned that I couldn't count on things being fair. That was the moment I realized that the measuring stick I needed to use was my own standards because they were all I could control.

Each year we had a school spelling bee, and that year I beat everyone in the third-grade (my grade) and fourth-grade classes to be the lone one standing at the end of the bee. I was elated and went home and practiced spelling aloud every word that my sister and mom would throw at me. Then I moved up to compete against the fifth- and sixth-grade classes. I held my own, and the school decided that those of us who were still standing would take on the big kids in the seventh and eighth grades. The seventh and eighth graders were in a different building, so we had to cross the schoolyard to get to that auditorium. I went out in an early round. I was disappointed, yet at the same time proud of my achievement. I was also confident that at the end of my third-grade year, I would win the spelling prize for my grade, so I worked hard to keep up the good work for the remainder of the school year.

When the prizes were being announced, I was ready to jump up and go forward when the teacher announced the spelling prize, but she announced another girl's name instead of mine. My classmates were shocked. I couldn't believe it! I was totally crushed; my eyes stung with tears, but I tried to pretend I didn't care.

When Mom picked me up from school, she asked how the day had gone, and I told her about the spelling prize, and I tried not to cry even though I felt cheated and didn't understand how I could prove that I could beat kids three classes ahead of me but see the top prize go to someone else.

My mom went up to school the next day and asked my teacher to explain why I hadn't won the award since I was clearly the best speller in the primary school. My teacher's response was, "I didn't feel that Veta needed to be recognized further. I thought another girl should be recognized and encouraged instead." That wasn't how the other prizes were awarded—they went to the student with the best performance, and I am sure my mother pressed that point to get an answer for why it was different for me.

I don't know what else that teacher said to Mom, but she must have communicated disrespect and prejudice because my mom came home, gave me a hug, and explained to me, "Veta, you didn't win the prize you deserved because you are a Black girl in a White school, and your teacher let her prejudice influence her decisions, and it made her disregard your achievements in favor of someone else." This was my first encounter with racism. I went to elementary school in the late 1960s and early 1970s when the Civil Rights era was still underway.

Looking back, I now understand why some kids didn't want to play with me and why I always seemed to stand out. It is bad enough when some of the kids leave you out, but when it is also their parents, your teachers, or other authorities, suddenly it sinks in deeply, because there's nothing you can do to change the color of your skin, or your ethnic heritage, or gender, or sexual orientation.

In 1963, Martin Luther King Jr. delivered his famous "I Have a Dream" speech. In it, he shared his vision for an America devoid of prejudice as well as segregation. I'm no MLK, but my vision is pretty broad, and it reflects the greater globalization of society we're experiencing today. In the world that I am working toward, people aren't limited by any of the ugly reasons that limit us now. Instead, everyone has the freedom to live where they want, to pursue their dreams and aspirations without boundaries or limits born out of bias or prejudice. And no matter who they are, no one looks at them and thinks that because they are _____ (you can fill in the blank with any kind of difference), they cannot be, do, or have what they want or be deprived of a fair chance to earn it.

It is my belief that all of our dreams and desires should be treated with respect and humanity, as should each of us as individuals. We are not there yet. I'm sure you have seen, heard, and probably experienced discrimination on the basis of your inherent characteristics. Even today we all know people who are Black or Brown, gay, transgender, female, or have disabilities... or are conspicuously different in other ways, who find themselves bullied, mocked, belittled, harassed, and limited. There are still countries where girls are deprived of education and seen as units of labor without dreams or aspirations of their own, and the list of injustices and prejudices could fill volumes. Even if you are straight, White, and male, I am betting you, too, know the sting of being on the outside or left out. Very few of us find that all doors of opportunity open wide for us. We all face difficulties that we need to overcome.

> **Very few of us find that all doors of opportunity open wide for us. We all face difficulties that we need to overcome.**

I don't merely want to succeed myself; I also want to make the world fairer and better for others, and I'm sure you do too. My hope is that by helping to empower you, you will be able to pay it forward and smooth the path that someone else will walk. It's that big dream that prompted me to pour hundreds of hours and considerable personal expense into writing this book.

WHERE THIS BOOK WILL TAKE YOU

This is a book about how you can take control of your own circumstances, whatever they happen to be, and create opportunities for yourself and also extend your ability to help others. At the age of eight, I learned that I was going to have to work harder, smarter, and more courageously if I wanted to fulfill my dreams. I faced the same choice then (and at other points along my journey) that you need to face now—to step up or to walk away from the challenge—and I believe that you owe it to yourself to go for it.

The six essential habits that I will outline in this book are universal principles that can be applied by anyone who wants to succeed but will be especially helpful when you encounter bias, stereotypes, discrimination, and other challenges. This first chapter will provide some context for the particular obstacles that I've faced that helped me formulate those principles. I don't think for a minute that my life is as tough as many others have had it because I have so much to be grateful for—especially a loving family, parents who believed in me, a sister who didn't hesitate to call me out when I needed it, supportive friends, and mentors to advise and counsel me.

WHAT FOUNDATION UNDERLIES MY SUCCESS

My grandmother was the first person on my father's side of the family to be born free—in Northumberland County, Virginia, the cradle of what had been the Confederacy. That almost takes my breath away whenever I think about it and imagine how difficult her life with my grandfather must have been in the rural south. My dad was one of eleven children, and one by one, his brothers and sisters supported one another to pursue college educations and move north in search of greater opportunities. Dad graduated from Temple University with a pharmaceutical degree and eventually opened his own pharmacy to serve the community in south Philadelphia. In just three generations, the Richardson family moved from enslavement to business owner to presidential advisor and CEO of a global organization.

Born in 1902 outside of Charleston, South Carolina, in a place called Summerville, my maternal grandmother was quite secretive about her early life. She told us she had no siblings, and all she ever told us about her parents is that they had died. Between 1904 and 1918, forty-two Black people were lynched in the state of South Carolina, and with that type of brutality and Jim Crow laws to boot, my grandmother's move to Philadelphia by herself in her early twenties seems an act born of both desperation and courage. She would marry a man who immigrated from the Philippines to Philadelphia following WWI. My grandfather died when my mother, the youngest, was about eighteen months old. My mother was fortunate to be able to finish high school, and she went straight to work afterward; college was beyond her reach. Mom was an amazing person: beautiful, fiercely loyal to her friends and family, and such an involved, loving, and encouraging mother. Every single day she communicated to my sister and me her 100 percent faith that we could do whatever we put our minds to doing. Whenever things didn't work out as we hoped, she helped us look at the situation, think about what we could have done differently, dust ourselves off, and try again. I sometimes wondered if her own unfulfilled ambition was behind her insistence that we both work so hard and aim so high. She was certainly acutely aware that a woman without a college degree, no matter how intelligent and hardworking, would experience limited opportunities, so she was determined that we were college bound.

My father used to sit us down and say, "In this family, we all have a job to do. My job is to work hard, serve customers, and bring in the money we need; your mother's job is to make sure you girls are clothed, fed, healthy, and comfortable; and you girls need to study hard and get good grades." I don't remember a time when I didn't know that was the way things worked, and we all accepted our assigned jobs. Dad worked late six days most weeks, either in the pharmacy serving customers, at home doing paperwork, or delivering prescriptions to less mobile customers after the pharmacy closed. Mom was always there to encourage us, to advocate for and spur her daughters onward, and to ensure that we were able to be self-sufficient in a way that she was not.

In my father's view, there were really only two acceptable career choices: doctor or lawyer. I soon decided that English and writing classes were more appealing than science, so I picked law. It's odd how our choices are made; I always knew that Mom loved me and accepted me 100 percent, no matter what I did, so while my mother shaped who I was, it was my father who directed what I would become. As a small business owner, he paid attention to commerce and read the *Wall Street Journal* diligently. I quickly discovered that if I asked him questions about business, I would get his attention, and that spurred my interest in corporations and commerce. I don't even remember a time when I didn't dream of being a lawyer in a *Fortune* 500 company, doing deals like those in the *Wall Street Journal*, and that was mostly because of my father's influence.

As two Black kids in a mostly White Catholic school, my sister and I always stood out, and Mom's influence ensured it was for positive reasons—our uniforms were meticulously cared for, we got top grades, we had good manners and participated in activities. I learned that I would have to earn every opportunity I wanted and that sometimes I still wouldn't receive the credit I deserved. I can't understate the power of my mom's advocacy, though. When I came home disappointed and ready to give up, her love and encouragement helped me get up again and keep going, and she would always do her best to find out what was going on and speak up for us. She unwittingly taught me the importance of identifying and eliminating the gaps so that there was no reason to pass me over.

College was just a stepping-stone. I was in a hurry to reach my real goal, which was law school, so I planned my undergraduate degree and graduated from the University of Maryland with a bachelor's of science in business management in just three years (normally an undergraduate degree in the United States takes four years of college to complete).

At last, I started my juris doctor at the University of Maryland Law School, and I had a great group of friends from a variety of backgrounds. In second year, when we studied constitutional law and affirmative action cases, there was a shift. During classroom discussion, someone inevitably would decide to grandstand about how unqualified Black students take seats that they do not deserve. Comments like "You are here because of affirmative action" were slipped in as a way of suggesting that I was not qualified. Well, my mom and my own past experience had taught me that there is a time when you need to stand up and speak up if you want to retain your own self-respect and be in a position to expect it from others. So while I may not have been top of the class, I did well enough to have a response ready: "If I'm not qualified to be here, then what does that say about you, since my grades are better than yours? Maybe you are the one who really shouldn't be here." I knew that I deserved to be there because I had worked hard to make it happen, and I wasn't going to let those comments pass. Learning to call out discriminatory comments and actions is a habit that has served me well on many occasions, as I called out both deliberate and unintentional racism directed toward me and also became an advocate for others in similar circumstances.

Every community has its own unique biases, and the legal community in the United States is no different: as an institution where White men have long held the majority of leadership positions to set the rules, it can be very difficult for others to feel as welcome and included. I will never forget the day when I was speaking at a legal conference and a woman came up to me afterward to share her story. I had spoken on diversity to the top leaders at the law firm where she worked as a junior associate at the time. As a result of the impact of that speech, she had the courage to speak up and acknowledge that she was a lesbian. Previously, she had felt that she had to hide that aspect of her identity as well as that of the woman she loved. After

The things we say can help be the catalyst for positive change.

my talk, which contributed to the firm's decision to expand its definition of diversity to include sexual orientation, she felt safer. She was open about it and found that being "out" did not affect her advancement, and she is now a successful law firm partner heading a practice group. I share this story to illustrate that her firm's leadership made changes because they wanted their workplace to be better, and the things we say can help be the catalyst for positive change.

After graduation, I spent the next eleven years of my career at Sunoco, learning my craft, meeting amazing people, and rising up through the legal ranks. By 1997, I was ready for change and a move back to the DC area. I applied for several positions and eventually landed as deputy general counsel of what was then called the American Corporate Counsel Association (now the Association of

Corporate Counsel, or ACC). It was a risky move to leave a big corporation with lots of resources and tens of thousands of employees for
a small nonprofit association of about thirty employees. Ironically,
the general counsel of Sunoco who hired me had been a founder of
ACC. People at Sunoco told me that it would be a big adjustment,
but the head of the law department was kind enough to offer that
they would hire me back if I did not like it, as long as it was within
two years. That safety net helped me leap to a very different role
with a lot more confidence. About one year later, I was promoted to
vice president. Not only did I love living in DC, but I also enjoyed the
entrepreneurial nature of my job and the opportunity to work on
important projects like Lawyers for One America, an initiative of the
Clinton administration intended to advance diversity and pro bono
service among legal professionals. Prior to this, my outspokenness
had been mostly on behalf of myself or others in my circle, but our
work on the Lawyers for One America team, which was led by then-
Deputy Attorney General Eric H. Holder Jr. (who would go on to serve
as attorney general under President Obama), aimed to advocate for
and actively promote greater racial and ethnic diversity in the legal
profession nationwide, so that our law schools, judiciary, law firms,
and corporations would become more diverse and inclusive. It was an
exciting opportunity for me as a woman of color, in a largely White,
male profession, to shape change.

A couple of years later, I was recruited by the Minority Corporate
Counsel Association (MCCA) as executive director. This was my chance
to be in charge; I was not yet forty years old, and I took it. Working
at MCCA was a challenge on many fronts and tested my ability to
overcome difficulties and believe in myself, but I relished the opportunity to become a diversity thought leader, and to give a hand through
scholarships, mentoring, education, networking, research reports, and

other initiatives designed to boost opportunities for diverse lawyers and law students. Several influential initiatives stand out from this time: a major research project that explored the behaviors women (in particular) exhibited that caused their careers to languish; an impactful study and report titled "Myth of the Meritocracy," which shed light on discrimination and bias in law firm hiring practices at the time; a program that actively recruited White male lawyers to participate and contribute their experiences to diversity programs as allies for underrepresented groups; and my work recruiting corporations to add their names to "friend of the court" filings in support of affirmative action cases at the US Supreme Court level. I am proud of the impact MCCA was able to make during my decade as its leader, and during this time, I was pleased to work with the Honorable Cari Dominguez, who chaired the US Equal Employment Opportunity Commission (EEOC) under President George W. Bush to support their innovative Freedom to Compete initiative, as well as to offer thoughts regarding potential candidates for nomination to the US Supreme Court at the invitation of President Barack Obama.

By 2011, I returned to ACC as president and CEO after undergoing a rigorous selection process. I succeeded my former boss, Fred Krebs, who was retiring after twenty years. Fred had been a supportive mentor over the years, and he remains a trusted advisor to this day. Going back to ACC felt a bit like returning home, and those colleagues from my earlier years at ACC warmly welcomed me back, offering a lesson about never burning bridges and being mindful of how you treat your coworkers. During my first three-year stint at ACC, I had started to formalize my practice of the habits I am going to share with you in this book. I quickly realized how instrumental they had been in shaping my experience, but it was during my years at MCCA and the analytical research we undertook that we codified and shared them widely. This research led to broader discussions with corporate executives who confirmed the observation that underrepresented groups (particularly women) did not do certain things in the corporate world as effectively or consistently as their White, straight, male counterparts. The first three principles—Take Stock, Take Risk, and Take Credit—were part of a more comprehensive set of career management recommendations issued as a report of findings from numerous interviews and informal surveys. While at MCCA, I led the development of a dozen first-of-their-kind research reports on diversity, and the association emerged as a knowledge center for innovative, best-in-class diversity/inclusion resources.

The more I thought about the truths I've learned, the more I realized how important it is to share the principles that I absorbed unconsciously. Not everyone has the same advantages that I have had: a dedicated mother, a hardworking father, a loving family that valued education, supportive colleagues and mentors, endless opportunities to learn to stand up for myself and others and develop the skills that would enable me to do this ... and much more.

The six habits that follow will help you to be ready when opportunity knocks.

And it starts with Take Stock: asking yourself where you want to go, examining where you are now, and making a plan to fill the gap between those two points, which is the topic of the next chapter.

IN CHAPTER 1 YOU DISCOVERED:

- Life isn't fair, and things don't always work out as you expect, so you need to prepare strategically if you want to advance your goals and dreams.

- Resilience, the ability to keep getting up and trying after being knocked down, is often more important than natural ability and talent.
- Once you know where you want to go, there are actions you can take, skills you can learn, and principles you can follow to overcome challenges and reach your destination faster.
- You will need help from others along the way, but you must also be prepared to help others too.
- You never know when you will have the opportunity to speak up and advocate for yourself or something you believe in. It is your responsibility to prepare for that day in every way possible.
- Looking back at where you have come from will help you get a clearer perspective on where you are now. This can be encouraging, especially if you don't feel that you are making progress.

TAKE SIX

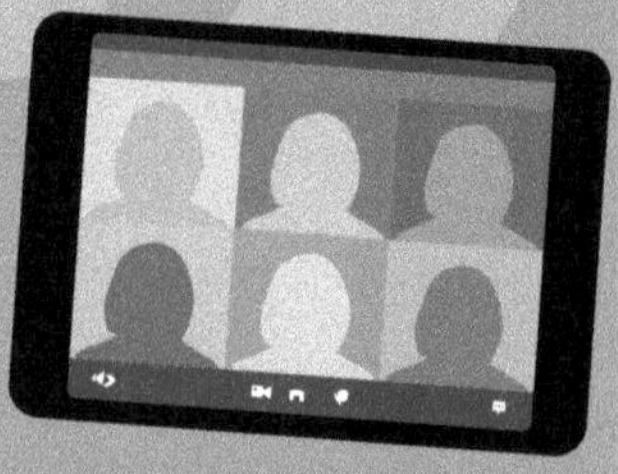

CHAPTER TWO

TAKE STOCK

If they don't give you a seat at the table, bring a folding chair.

—SHIRLEY CHISHOLM

Undergraduate degree in business management? Check.
Good score on LSAT? Check.
Get into a well-respected law school? Check.
Legal internship at a *Fortune* 500 corporation ... oh no!

What could I do to check off that milestone?

During my second year of law school, along with my peers, I was looking for a summer internship. However, I had a problem: unlike most of my classmates, I was seeking a career in corporate law, and the only employers who came to the University of Maryland were representatives of the big law firms and a few government agencies. There wasn't a single corporation among them. I could have settled for an internship in one of the law firms or government, but my heart was set on fulfilling my childhood dream of working at the kind of company I had read about in the *Wall Street Journal* and discussed with my father; after all, that had been the impetus behind my undergraduate degree in business management.

In a way, it was an easy decision. When I started my juris doctor, I had planned those three years out. My plans included a corporate internship; my challenge was turning that plan into reality.

It was the 1980s, well before the internet made searching for companies and the names and contact details of individuals within easy access. I scoured available alumni lists, corporate annual reports, and SEC filings, looking for companies with large legal departments. I went to the law school career placement office, ransacked the library for directories that would help me find the names and addresses I needed, and started writing persuasive letters that explained who I was, what I wanted, and humbly asked, "Would you have an opportunity for me to work with you for the summer to gain experience working in the field of corporate law?"

Then I waited.

I received some rejections. Many of my letters were simply ignored. I had no real leads. My level of anxiety grew. What if I didn't get an internship at all that summer? Most of the positions at law firms were already filled. Was I chasing a mirage?

One of my friends, whose father worked at Sunoco, told me that they hired law students and had an internship program. I knew Sunoco, of course—what Philadelphia girl didn't in those days? It was definitely on my list of dream places I'd like to work, so I looked up the Sunoco general counsel's name, reviewed my letter, and sent it, along with my résumé, to Donald P. Walsh. Then I waited for a response.

Don Walsh was a very busy executive, but like many good leaders, he understood the importance of investing in future generations, which was why he had started a summer internship program to do just that. Back in those days, the sort of program Sunoco offered was really quite innovative and unique. The time between my letter of inquiry and the response felt like forever. Finally, the letter of reply arrived in my mailbox. I saw the Sunoco logo on the envelope, my heart leaped with expectation, and I took the letter back to my room, took a deep breath, and tore open the envelope. It was a gracious letter, but it dashed all my hopes. There was no mistaking the clarity of this rejection: all five positions were already filled, and Sunoco only hired interns from local Philadelphia-area law schools.

What next?

I took stock of my options. Sunoco was the only way forward if I wanted to take the shortest route toward my dream. I simply had no other internship options at any other corporate law department, and to apply for a corporate legal job straight out of law school without any prior exposure was unlikely to succeed. I also convinced myself that this rejection was the result of policy and budget issues more than anything else. In a company the size of Sunoco, there would be no shortage of work that law-student interns could complete. I just needed to plot my strategy to get inside and try to prove my worth.

What price was I willing to pay?

I wrote back to Don and thanked him for his response. Then I went on to explain that this was my childhood dream that I had been working toward through college and law school. It was so important to me that I was willing to spend my summer working for free as an unpaid intern just to gain the experience I needed.

He was impressed enough to have a deputy set up a call with me. Before mobile phones, this meant organizing a date and time to call on a landline, and at the end of the call, I was offered an unpaid internship for the summer. I was on my way to checking off another milestone!

That was how, at the end of my second year of law school, I swallowed my pride, moved home to live with my parents, slept in my small childhood bedroom, and made my way to Sunoco on the first day of my internship, outwardly composed but inwardly trembling. It was also how, at the start of my final year of law school, I made history at Sunoco: I was the only walk-on to ever be offered a position upon graduation, one of only two graduates they hired that year, and she and I remain good friends to this day.

WHAT DOES IT MEAN TO "TAKE STOCK"?

The *Merriam-Webster Dictionary* defines "taking stock" (of something) as "to think carefully about a situation or event and form an opinion about it, so that you can decide what to do." While that definition is perfectly adequate, it doesn't truly reflect the life-changing potential that Take Stock offers when you create a habit of using it to shape your dreams into your reality. Maya Angelou said, "I believe that the most important single thing, beyond discipline and creativity, is daring to dare." The habit Take Stock helps us to see what skills we need to develop and what creative action we need to take in order to reach the ambitious goals we dare to set ourselves.

The habit Take Stock involves defining and refining your goals: you might start, as I did, with the idea of being a lawyer, and then narrow it down to a career in corporate law and then branch out later, or you might start with a very specific goal and later realize that you are interested in something quite different. Once you have a clear goal (whether it is broad or narrow), though, you need to look at where you are and where you want to end up, and measure what you will need to do to bridge the gap. This is not a measuring stick to beat yourself up with but a compass to guide you toward success.

Sometimes, as I discovered when I was seeking an internship at Sunoco, taking stock means finding out whether "No" really means "No," or if it means something else, like "Not now" or "Not based on the existing information" or even "Not as far as I'm concerned!" Proactively, to Take Stock means plotting your course of action so you can exert greater control over your own destiny. Occasionally, when you Take Stock, you may realize that you're pursuing a goal that is no longer right for you, but mostly you're using this habit to serve as a course-correction tool to stay on track and speed up your progress.

In this chapter, we'll look at this essential habit from many angles so that you can see the variety of ways in which it can help you uncover unexpected opportunities, discover innovative solutions, and apply your energy and talent to achieving what you really want, even when people all around you tell you that it can't be done.

TAKING STOCK HAPPENS DAILY AND MAKES A DIFFERENCE

I was fortunate enough to live in a family where the need to Take Stock was part of our DNA and was applied in every area of our lives, from big life-direction decisions to more frivolous or mundane decisions. My parents set an example for me. My father would Take Stock of his business and cash flow, my mother would Take Stock and manage our household, and I was expected to use this as a tool to plan my studies, household chores, and social commitments. It is one of those habits that grows more natural as you use it until it becomes second nature, both as a compass to help you realize your dreams and an anchor when the unexpected disrupts your life.

Long before I went to college, I became proficient at taking stock, and I even overcame being shy and socially awkward by plotting conversational flowcharts to map out how to hold up my end of a phone call and avoid uncomfortable silences or to discover whether a particular boy had a romantic interest in me or was just being friendly. It could have been just a fun and frivolous exercise that I laughed over with my sister, but it was also the foundation for our futures as we mapped out our lives and dreams. Either way, the habit helped me sharpen the important skills needed for bigger decisions and life choices.

> **It is also important to think about how you will close that gap between where you are and where you wish to end up and break it into a series of small steps, especially when the divide is very wide.**

Over the years, it has become very clear that this habit has been a powerful gift that is effective on both a personal and organizational level. It doesn't completely remove the anxiety and stress that is an integral part of having high goals, but it does direct that nervousness toward constructive action. I've noticed that very few people apply this practice consistently and effectively long term, and I believe that the failure to do so is one reason people may lose their motivation, direction, and enthusiasm. It is also important to think about how you will close that gap between where you are and where you wish to end up and break it into a series of small steps, especially when the divide is very wide. It's like that old saying: "How do you eat an elephant? One bite at a time!"

LOOKING PAST OTHERS' EXPECTATIONS AND FOCUSING ON YOUR OWN GOALS

I recently attended a reception held on Zoom to celebrate the accomplishments of a group of students from Houston, Texas, who were selected as scholars for a very special program. The evening's keynote speaker was the Honorable Vanessa Gilmore, a federal court judge who spoke about having courage to pursue your dreams. Judge Gilmore quoted her mother's sage advice to her as Judge Gilmore pursued her legal career: "Don't get on the fast train to someone else's destiny." In essence, the advice was to pursue **your own** dreams. How very powerfully that sums it up!

Take Stock requires you to spend the time to clarify your goals and dreams for yourself and to be honest with yourself about them. You must look into your own heart for those things that will be personally satisfying or professionally fulfilling for you rather than trying to fulfill another's expectations, whether that person is a parent, sibling, partner, spouse, or child. You want to listen to your inner voice and answer as truthfully as possible such questions as these:

- What do I really want?
- How do I envision my life?
- What will make me happy?
- How do I wish to contribute?
- How do I wish to spend my time?

This doesn't mean that you ignore other people's advice, wishes, and wise counsel; it does mean that you take responsibility for your own choices, though. I started off by falling in line with my father's expectations and elected to pursue a career in law, but along the way it became my passion, my hope, and my dream, and it is a choice I have never regretted. I know other people who initially fell into line with their parents' wishes (or in some cases, the parents' unfulfilled dreams) and later realized that they were following a path that didn't suit them, or that their initial interest had waned. Taking stock would help them to see the lack of alignment, reevaluate their choices, and move in new directions that were a better fit for them.

If you don't know where you are going, then it doesn't matter which road you take; you'll remain lost.

I have noticed that it's especially common to find accomplished people pursuing careers in law and medicine because these fields are prestigious or because of family tradition, more for the sake of their parents than because they care about that field themselves. That may be enough to carry you through the initial years, when the excitement of admission to your field, gaining financial independence, and starting a new job provides its own satisfaction and challenges, but some years in, many of these people are counting the years and months to retirement. I think that is terribly sad, and it undermines the vision of everyone being able to exercise their gifts and abilities and be themselves.

ULTIMATELY, IT IS UP TO YOU TO SET THE DIRECTION

If you don't know where you are going, then it doesn't matter which road you take; you'll remain lost. But once you know what you want, then you are in a position to evaluate your options, shape your destiny, and plan the specific steps you need to reach your destination.

When I first went to the University of Maryland to complete my undergraduate degree in business management, I saw that solely as a stepping-stone to my real goal: a juris doctor and a career in corporate law. My goal was to complete that undergraduate degree as quickly as possible so that I could move on to the next stage of my career, and I'd heard of people who had graduated from college in three years rather than the standard four, so I went looking for advice to help me plan my undergraduate degree with that in mind.

My first step was a meeting with one of the university's guidance counselors to map out my accelerated course of study. That meeting didn't go quite the way that I expected. I walked into her office as a brand-new freshman, anticipating that she would have looked at my transcript, would listen to my goals, and actively help me plan my moves. I walked out disappointed, frustrated, yet wiser.

My guidance counselor was completely uninterested in my goals, my reasons for pursuing them, or even my existing record of achievements. When I talked about my desire to complete my degree within three years, she looked at me as though I were sharing my intention to compete in an Olympic event for which I had never previously trained. She also tried to discourage me and advised that I should not be so ambitious and lower my sights. She hadn't even looked at my transcript! That would be the first and last time I visited my guidance counselor. Although her discouraging response didn't cause me to waver regarding my ambitions, it did mean that I needed to look around for other students who were fast-tracking their undergraduate courses and use their advice and expertise to determine what I needed to do to achieve my goal by objectively assessing

- my current situation;
- my objectives; and

- my timeline.

My best friend, Cheryl Thompson, was a sophomore that year. Cheryl and I met as ivies (i.e., pledgees) for Alpha Kappa Alpha Sorority, Inc., and she had already designed her own program so that she could graduate in three years. With her guidance, I proceeded to chart my own courses, which included certain summer school classes so that I could graduate a year early. We both knew what needed to be done and followed the route we had plotted with regular check-ins and occasional course corrections along the way. Like Cheryl, I finished college a year early and immediately went to law school just as she had done.

WHY TAKE STOCK?

If you are reading this book, I'm confident that you are ambitious, determined to take control of your life, and willing to work hard to achieve your goals once you have determined what they are. That means that you have many, many opportunities available, and you're probably good at a number of things. That also means that you have choices to make about where you will focus your efforts. When I chose to become a lawyer rather than a doctor, it wasn't because my grades in science and math weren't good; it was because I preferred to focus on language arts. Similarly, when I chose to pursue a corporate legal career, it wasn't because I couldn't get a job at a law firm (in fact, that would have been the easy option); it was a deliberate choice based upon my dreams and strengths. However, it was a choice that I would not have made if I hadn't been in touch with my own goals.

There are a lot of people in this world who will encourage you to take the well-trodden path or sell you short without really listening or learning about you. If you don't take control of your life, then others will do it for you, and I can guarantee that you likely won't like the result. Drive your own life and career. Don't go along for someone else's ride, or as Judge Gilmore's mother wisely advised, don't take that fast train to someone else's destiny. Take ownership of your destiny.

At Sunoco, during that important summer internship opportunity, I met a woman who took me under her wing and who mentored and encouraged me from then onward. Ann Mulé was one of few people apart from Don Walsh and his deputies who knew that I was basically volunteering that summer. I didn't want anyone to ask less of me or treat me differently because I wasn't being paid; I was following my dream and planned on giving it all I had, and Ann reinforced that was the best way to approach the summer. Ann encouraged me throughout that summer to be my authentic self. She was a young, fun, spirited daughter of second-generation Italian immigrants who instilled in me her own strong work ethic and empathy for others. Through that summer and beyond, she set an example of an effective and busy person who was very generous with her assistance and advice whenever she saw junior lawyers who were committed to their goals. The one piece of advice she gave that had the most impact on me was, "When you are being your authentic self, not trying to imitate someone else, then you are more relatable and genuine, and that is you at your most powerful."

If you don't know who you are or what you want, then you are giving up your "magic powers" and playing down your own strengths.

That's an important reason to Take Stock. If you don't know who you are or what you want, then you are giving up your "magic powers" and playing down your own strengths.

I'm not the first person to realize that the attributes that, in some ways, seemed to spur my biggest challenges were actually my greatest strengths. For example, as a Black girl in an all-White school I wouldn't and couldn't simply blend in, so I learned to stand out in positive ways ... and to stand up for myself as well as for others who needed a boost or an advocate. I also had no choice but to speak up and learn how to deal with difficult situations and difficult people. The result was that I developed navigational skills and resilience that those who spend their lives as part of a majority may lack or take longer to acquire. Part of taking stock is assessing your strengths as well as your weaknesses or vulnerabilities so that you can amplify the former and overcome the latter. For me, being both Black and female provides the foundation from which I draw strength, even though it sometimes makes my path harder to navigate.

THE CONNECTION BETWEEN VISUALIZING YOUR GOALS AND YOUR OUTCOMES

In a literal sense, most businesses Take Stock at least once each year in order to

- measure the goods they have on hand and find out which are selling well and which are moving slowly;

- uncover discrepancies between what they think they have and what they actually have in inventory; and

- evaluate their pricing and profits in relation to sources of revenue.

There's a very practical reason for this habit: these annual check-ins provide the business with accurate information about their progress toward profit and market goals. Similarly, when you Take Stock in your personal and professional life, you are better able to measure your goals, continually evaluate your progress, and stay on track to achieve your objectives.

Academic disciplines including behavioral economics, cognitive science, and neuropsychology have analyzed the powerful effect that visualizing yourself in the reality that you want to create has on your behavior. Elite athletes are taught to see themselves successfully crossing the finish line and hearing the roar of the crowd because the act of visualizing your accomplishment has an effect on your mind and your body. It also helps you to see what needs to change in order for you to achieve your goals, **and** it releases endorphins, the powerful, feel-good chemicals that increase motivation and pleasure even while you are completing the difficult and possibly dull routines that are necessary to become a champion. NASCAR drivers, fighter pilots, jockeys, and high-achieving athletes have long been trained to look where they want to go, and that if they look at the wall, the car, the opponent, or the plane in front of them, that is what they will hit. Neuroscience is only now getting to the point where it can measure the brain activity that triggers your reflexes and demonstrates how your mental picture actually determines your actions and movements.[1]

In 1979, the Harvard Business School MBA graduating class was asked the question, "Have you set written goals and created a plan for their attainment?" Prior to graduation, it was determined that 84 percent of the class had set no goals at all; a total of 13 percent had set written goals but had no concrete plans; and 3 percent had both written goals and concrete plans. Twenty years later, the 13 percent

---

1   For more on the neuroscience behind this, see "Additional Resources" at http://www.TakeSixHabits.com/.

of the class that had set written goals but had not created plans were making twice as much money as the 84 percent of the class that had set no goals at all, and the 3 percent that had both written goals and a plan were making ten times as much as the other 97 percent of the class.[2] This demonstrates the incredible momentum that you can use to drive your behavior and accelerate your results when you take the time to not only write down your goals, but also plan the steps and milestones you will reach along the way. Evaluating your progress only speeds things up.

WHEN SHOULD YOU TAKE STOCK?

The short answer to this question is "as often as possible," because you are never done changing, growing, evolving, and adapting. More specifically, the answer is you should Take Stock at least every six months, and more frequently when you are pursuing a challenging goal or thinking about transition. During times of extreme and rapid change, such as we experienced as a result of COVID-19 and the challenges that have been offshoots of the global pandemic (health, safety, financial, professional, political, societal), you may be taking in new information daily and taking stock at the end of every day as you prepare for whatever may be coming next.

You are changing, and the world is changing rapidly around you, so it's important to keep your finger on the pulse of your goals, desires, and opportunities and recognize when they have changed or should change. This constant state of flux creates a level of anxiety that the process of taking stock helps you keep under control, because it gives

---

2   Mark H. McCormack, *What They Don't Teach You at Harvard Business School* (Bantam, 1986).

you a framework that you can work from and oversee. Being in control lessens anxiety and will ultimately be comforting.

I decided quite early that my future lay in corporate law, and my process to Take Stock has always been focused on the next step within that framework—always working with or in the corporate business sector. Other people work differently. My longtime friend Mike Pearson parlayed his intelligence and athletic ability to the Ivy League and a scholarship at the University of Pennsylvania. After graduating, Mike also set his sights on going to law school and landed at the University of Michigan, one of the top-ranked law schools in the United States. Two years in, Mike took stock and realized law wasn't for him. The legal world was not where he wanted to spend his professional life, so he dropped out after his second year and joined the military, against the well-meaning advice of most of his friends and family, who urged him to complete that third year and get his law degree since he would still have to pay off his student loans. After several years of service, including a stint in the Persian Gulf, Mike started the first of several successful businesses. Today, he's a serial entrepreneur and investor, sits on corporate boards, and is a wealthy man. More importantly, he's satisfied with the course his life has taken, and entrepreneurship suits him in a way that the buttoned-down nature of legal work did not.

Another friend of mine, BK Fulton, had a successful and fulfilling career as a top executive at Verizon Communications. As he took stock, the time came when he realized that he was ready for a new challenge and ultimately determined to produce films and launch several media and entertainment ventures. Over the next few years BK assessed the gaps, assembled a team to supplement his own talents, and in 2017, he started a film company, Soulidifly Productions—in many ways a far cry from his role at Verizon, but in step with his changing personal vision.

Without a regular practice of evaluation and assessment, BK might never have taken on this new challenge, which has brought him great satisfaction, success, and new opportunities to make a difference in the world.

Many professionals Take Stock once a year—when it's time for their annual performance review. This is better than nothing, but it is not really enough to reach the heights of achievement or to stay in touch with your personal goals. You can see this clearly when you think about the purpose of Take Stock: to decide what your goal is, what stands between you and your goal, and what needs to happen (consider these your interim objectives) so that you reach your goal as quickly as possible.

Clearly, at different times of your life and career, you need to Take Stock and measure your progress more frequently, and at other times you can and may need to stretch it out.

When I started pursuing my business management degree, I had already planned my next six years out (to the end of my JD) on a semester-by-semester basis (including summers), although I needed the help of my best friend to understand fully what steps to take. In addition to the core courses in which I planned to enroll and the internships and experience I needed, I had a growing list of skills that I would have to develop. This list was prepared on the basis of reading, listening, and learning from others about what it would take to become the corporate counsel to a *Fortune* 500 company and do big transactions. As I went along, I would fill in the details, add new items, and reorder those skills, but I always had a rough outline to follow and a purposeful focus. Once I got my first job at Sunoco, I eagerly learned as much as I could about the business, the players, how to ask for opportunities, and whom to ask for information. As far as possible, I left nothing to chance.

The need to Take Stock doesn't just apply to individuals; it also applies to companies. The moment I walked into my office at MCCA on my first day as executive director, I knew that I had a massive task ahead of me (and that I probably hadn't asked the right questions prior to accepting the role—I had failed to Take Stock to take a hard look at MCCA's financial health). I'll never forget the words of MCCA's external accountant my first week on the job: "I have good news and bad news," he said, "so what would you like to hear first?" When I replied that I would take the good news first, he replied, "Well, the good news is that there is a total of $4,000 in the operating account, and the bad news is there's insufficient funds to meet payroll on the fifteenth, so you need to decide what to do." The organization was effectively insolvent, and we would have to draw from an unsecured line of credit in order to meet payroll.

I shut my door, took out a sheet of paper, and started to Take Stock by looking at every area of the organization, all aimed at for-mulating the strategy to turn MCCA's debt-laden situation around. I was already familiar with the mission statement and general goals, but it was time to look at the specifics and the initial list of questions to which answers would be critical:

- Finances, especially accounts receivable and payable: Who owed MCCA, and whom did MCCA owe?

- Staff: Who did what? How would they need to refocus to bring in revenue and maintain key supporter relationships?

- Membership: What relationships could we draw upon and tout? Who might be "fast wins to join" and remit member-ship dues?

- Board of directors: What did they need to know, and what call to action would they be given?

- Sponsors and donors: Who are the VIP contributors? What are the points of connection between members, board directors, and sponsors, and how do we leverage these to raise funds as well as help hold certain creditors at bay?

- Past activities: What was the history of MCCA's programs and events—which were financial winners, and which were losers? Were they losers as a result of mismanagement that could be corrected, or was it better to cut them loose and develop new ones?

- Planned activities: What revenue opportunities were on the horizon, and what does success for these events look like?

- Other resources and allies: What other current assets or relationships are not being fully tapped?

At the start of this book, I reflected on my feelings of total inadequacy during my summer internship at Sunoco. That whole summer I was just waiting for someone to stand up and say, "You don't belong here," and send me home. This time, the challenge was even greater... but now, I had had several years of professional experience negotiating the purchases and sales of businesses, doing financial due diligence, assessing liabilities, and mitigating risk, and I had the strategic ability to see past the barriers to the opportunity beyond the bend. I started with the cold, hard facts of the current situation and began to map out my own vision for MCCA in the coming month, three months, six months, one year, eighteen months, and more. Then, focusing on the immediate needs at month one, I looked at the gaps that I had already discovered and thought about how to fill them, along with the conversations with creditors and supporters that I needed to personally initiate as the new executive director. Despite the financial mess that I had inherited, I had also inherited a solid foundation from which to build. That, in combination with a clear vision and a plan for advancing it, enabled me to know, deep down and with reasonable confidence, that the situation was manageable and that I could lead its turnaround.

As we faced down one wave of emergencies after another those first months, taking stock was a daily activity for myself and my small team. There was so much to do, and each of us had to determine which things would deliver the greatest impact and close the biggest gaps. We all had areas in which we needed to grow and develop new skills, as well as simply get things done. It's funny how flying without a safety net enables your wings to strengthen and take flight.

> It's funny how flying without a safety net enables your wings to strengthen and take flight.

HOW DO YOU TAKE STOCK?

You've already read several scenarios in which I took stock to ensure that I was poised to take advantage of the next opportunity to advance my objectives. I've added them because the power of this process lies in the specific application to your circumstances and because I want to demonstrate that these habits will work for you just as they did for me.

The basics of "How to Take Stock" for any aspect of your career, relationships, or other area of life is quite simple:

1. Honestly assess where you are at present: Where am I now?

2. Determine where you want to go in as vivid detail as possible because, as you have seen, a clear vision creates clarity, persistence, and momentum: Where do I want to be?

3. Discover what skills, qualifications (including education or training), and experience you need to fill the gap: What is required to bridge the divide between where I am and where I want to be?

4. Find role models from whom you can learn: Who has done something similar, and how can I learn from them? What mistakes did they make that I can avoid? What publications or resources are must-reads for them to stay up to date? Which industry groups, professional societies, or networks do they participate in?

5. Ask for feedback from those around you: What am I missing that other people can identify? How do they see me?

6. If you are ready but your gap is that the right opportunity has yet to come your way, then how are you going to reposition yourself in order to earn that chance to prove your worth? Will you need to raise your profile and become better known in your sector? Are there executive recruiters you need to connect with? Whom can you trust to share your desire to make a next move? The more people who are looking and listening out for you, the greater your chance of hearing about the right opportunity.

You need to be brutally honest with yourself throughout this process, but don't rely only on your own assessment of where you are now and what it will take to fill the gap. Other people's honest feedback is extremely important as well, especially feedback from people who are already where you aspire to be and those who are ahead of you on the path. They can help you see your shortcomings in a way that you cannot see on your own. They can also help you assess the qualifications you will need in a professional context. We'll talk more about the importance of this kind of guidance and specifics about how to seek it in chapter 5, "Take a Hand."

THE SKILL OF GIVING AND RECEIVING FEEDBACK

A key skill that you must develop is the ability to receive honest feedback without defensiveness, ask appropriate clarification questions where needed, and evaluate the relevance of the feedback later. This skill is based on the reality that the person giving you feedback is usually trying to help you with their honest assessment, not trying to erode your confidence and pull you down. As a leader, you will also need to learn how to give valuable feedback to members of your team or staff, so it is useful to pay attention to how others deliver it to you and copy the best approaches you experience.

One of the significant discoveries that came out of the research we did at MCCA was that women, especially women of color, were rarely given the same level of specific, direct, and honest feedback as White men and that this held them back from taking the actions they needed to progress. There are many reasons for this, but basically, the bottom-line cause is some sort of discomfort within the relationship. It has been reported that some women are more concerned than their male counterparts about being liked and perceived as nice, and this can result in their reluctance to deliver "needs improvement" feedback to others because of concern over being perceived as mean, not nice, or unlikable.[3] This is a significant problem because we all have blind spots, and if no one points them out to us, we cannot choose whether to address them or not.

The MCCA research focused specifically on women, and the issue it recognizes has been confirmed repeatedly in conversations with many leaders from a variety of industries. Studies also indicate that this is an issue for racial/ethnic/LGBTQ+ minorities as well, who are often provided with overly lenient and nonspecific feedback, possibly because the feedback provider does not want to be considered racist, homophobic, or otherwise insensitive.[4] Generous or nonspecific feedback may be motivated by a desire to avoid tears, conflict, confrontation, and accusations of discrimination, but it doesn't serve you if your goal is to move upward. Therefore, my belief has always been that it is my job to make the evaluator comfortable enough to give it to me straight and that I have to avoid wincing, even if it stings, to hear how I need to improve.

One of my former colleagues, Jane Pigott, managed a team member at her law firm whose work as an associate was solid but whose attitude and social skills left a lot to be desired. He would not look people in the eye, didn't follow through on certain tasks she assigned, and failed to acknowledge his coworkers in the hallway, even when they spoke to him to say hello. In short, he lacked emotional intelligence and people-related skills, and overall, this reflected badly on the whole group. When he was nominated for partner, it was Jane's task to tell him that he hadn't received sufficient votes. She could

---

3   For studies showing this, see http://www.TakeSixHabits.com/.

4   See, for instance, K. D. Harber, "Feedback to Minorities: Evidence of a Positive Bias," *Journal of Personality and Social Psychology* 74, no. 3 (1998): 622-28; and Alyssa Croft and Toni Schmader, "The Feedback Withholding Bias: Minority Students Do Not Receive Critical Feedback from Evaluators Concerned about Appearing Racist," *Journal of Experimental Social Psychology* 48 no. 5 (2012): 1139-44.

have simply told him the results without taking the additional step to share why. However, she was generous enough to tell him the truth: "Here are the areas in which you are deficient, and to make partner, you need me to recommend you for it and advocate for you, but I will not support your consideration for partner until you address these issues and convince me you have changed."

It wasn't easy for Jane to meet one on one with this man and give him negative feedback as well as the news that he had been passed over, but it was an act of kindness nevertheless. She gave him specific examples and advice about what needed to change. From that point, the ball was in his court. He had the information he needed to decide what his next move would be: to stay the same and be again passed over, to move to another firm, or to change his behavior (eventually he moved to another firm, and we lost track of his progress). Jane used a term I had never heard before, "the gift of feedback," to describe the generosity of her action. Some hear that term and scoff at the idea that a person could view negative criticism as being generous, but I agree wholeheartedly with Jane that is exactly what it is, and I adopt the term myself when I want to invest in someone who has promise but a few issues to address.

I have been on the receiving end of that kind of feedback as well. My instinctive response is to react with denial and explanations. However, I have learned how important it is to just shut up and listen rather than fight or negate it. Feedback is, after all, essential information that I need to hear and evaluate if I want to move forward, so even when it hurts, it is still a gift to be treated with care and gratitude. I try to keep that in mind when I'm giving feedback as well, because the goal of feedback is to give people important information that will help them grow and progress.

Natalie was a highly competent woman who worked at one of

my workplaces. She had started at an entry level and worked her way up to a position of significant responsibility, and now she wanted to move up even further. We were keen to help her with that, but there was a problem: she had a very transactional approach. Give Natalie a problem to solve, and she did an excellent job of breaking it down into tasks that could be completed and checked off, but ask her to think about policy, implications, and the bigger picture, and she was way out of her depth. It wasn't simply that she didn't have the skills required. We were happy to coach her on those, but even when we gave her the next opportunity, she could not connect the dots from prior experiences or lessons learned and demonstrate an aptitude for growth. I shared the responsibility of explaining our assessment with her, and it was hard. I really wanted to take the coward's way out and skirt around the issue, but that wouldn't have been fair to Natalie, so I laid out the situation for her: she had had several tries, and we just couldn't see her moving to the next level. In fact, I was not alone in the belief that absent a turnaround effort, she would likely never be able to handle that style of nonlinear thinking, so she had topped out and would not be promoted to the next level. I also told her that we appreciated her work where she was and that she was more than welcome to stay in her current role.

Soon after, Natalie left for another organization where she negotiated a better title, a chance to reset relationships and expectations, and a fresh opportunity to prove herself. She left on good terms, and the last I heard she was doing well—far better than she would have been doing if she had stayed where she was and continued being passed over. Honesty with Natalie was critical because it put her in the driver's seat to make choices about her own career rather than wasting years wondering why that promotion was still not coming her way.

TAKING STOCK AND DEVELOPING SKILLS

In addition to the qualifications and experience that you'll identify as you Take Stock, you'll also run into some important social and life skills that are harder to quantify. Sometimes, I meet people who make comments like, "I'm an introvert, so I will never be good at networking" or "I don't communicate well from a stage." My response is to remind them that people, especially smart people like them who have big goals and dreams, can develop whatever skills they need for success if they choose to do so.

Many people fear public speaking more than anything. Jen, a young event planner I worked with while I was at MCCA, was one of those people. She was immensely talented but liked to stay way behind the scenes out of sight and was particularly shy about standing on the platform and making announcements or being visible in any way. I could see her potential but could also see that she was standing in her own way, so I took stock on her behalf and decided to nudge her ability to acquire the skills that she was clearly capable of learning. We had a few conversations about her ambitions, and she was too bright and coachable not to make progress, but I knew that as long as she hid from standing on a stage in front of people and speaking, her advancement to full potential was unlikely. Over the next few years, little by little I pushed her onto the stage: first to make announcements, and then to make introductions, and later to fill in gaps when something unexpected occurred and someone—Jen—needed to step up and fill in. It wasn't long before she overcame her fear of public speaking and developed this important skill. In all honesty, I do not really know if Jen actually overcame her fear or simply learned to work around it. That really doesn't matter now; she's capable and can effectively handle opportunities to stand up front. In fact, she does such a good job that others invite her to present at their events. As a mentor, it is always gratifying to see someone realize that if she can just change her perspective and develop that particular skill, nothing is out of her reach. One day, assuming it's what she wants, she'll seek to be an executive director, and I'll happily support that ambition.

Many who have watched me network in a room filled with people would find it hard to believe that I am naturally an introvert and used to find it very awkward to make conversation with strangers. While I was still in law school, I realized that this "networking" was a skill that would be just as critical to my future success as my course selection and subject mastery would be, so I set out to learn how to network successfully. This was hard work, but I approached it like everything else—I was disciplined and put myself "in training," pursuing a similar strategy to the one that I later worked on with Jen.

In order to practice my networking skills, I would set a goal to attend a particular networking event with a group of professionals outside the legal and corporate fields so that there was no danger that someone would remember me as the socially inept woman or, while interviewing me for a job opportunity, recall the awkward conversations they had with me years prior at an industry event. Each time, I entered the event with a goal to speak to a certain number of people (starting small with just three people, and gradually increasing the number). Then the length of the interactions had to meet certain milestones. I prepared in advance, mapping the conversation in my head just as I had as a teenager before social events. I planned my brief introduction, prepared some questions designed to draw other people out, and studied some information that was relevant to the kind of people at the event (nurses, accountants, teachers, and so forth) that I could share. As soon as I had completed a specific number of conversations (no matter how they went or how long that took), I was free to leave.

My first attempt was painful! I arrived at the event alone, feeling as though I was both conspicuous and invisible at the same time. I had briefly considered going along with a friend but decided that I didn't want anyone to witness my total ineptitude. Plus, having a friend would mean I'd lean on her instead of learning to navigate on my own.

"OK, Veta," I said to myself, "you've got to have three conversations. Then you can leave, and the chances are that you'll never see any of these people again."

I took a deep breath and walked up to someone who was standing alone, reached out to shake hands, introduced myself, asked where she was from, and even managed a few extra sentences. A few minutes later, the conversation was over, and I was again looking for someone to meet. Twice more that evening, I walked up to someone, introduced myself, and stumbled through some awkwardly superficial questions and conversational gambits. It was such a relief when, finally, I had completed my assignment and could head back home feeling numb and mentally drained from the stress. Slowly, the number of conversations I challenged myself to have at each event crept up, and it started to feel like a game, not a penance. The next challenge was to improve on the quality of the conversation and expand the range of topics. Gradually, I discovered that I was mastering this networking thing and started to enjoy myself and feel a sense of accomplishment. My ability to relate and carry on conversations with total strangers was growing, and it was totally because I put myself in training.

Eventually, I gained the confidence to attend legal and corporate events. Today, you can drop me into a room filled with strangers anywhere in the world, and I am comfortable carrying conversations and even connecting other strangers, but it didn't happen on its own, and it is certainly not an innate skill. It was the result of a careful analysis of where my networking skills were compared with where they needed to be, followed by equally careful planning of the steps and actions required to close the gap, combined with consistent practice to perfect the skill, or at least develop a high level of competence.

A few years ago, when the American Bar Association published the first edition of Susan R. Sneider's *A Lawyer's Guide to Networking*, a very useful resource for lawyers (and other professionals) who want to develop networking skills, she shared my story as an example of a model networker whose example people could follow in learning the social skills required to navigate successfully. When Susan first reached out to ask if she could include my story, she told me that she had been asking around in order to build a list of some of the best networkers in the legal profession and that my name kept being suggested. I was floored. Honestly, if you were able to observe my first efforts in this area, you would realize that none of us is born with an A game, but it is possible to learn whatever skills you need once you have identified the gap that needs to be filled and are motivated to want to close that gap. If I can learn to network effectively, anyone who puts their mind to it can develop similar skills.

WHAT DO I DO, NOW THAT I KNOW WHAT I KNOW?

Taking stock is something that I do regularly in every area of my life because it's such a powerful assessment tool. I use it as both a compass and a prod: it tells me in what direction I need to move and how to fill the gap. It also helps me see when it's time to change my direction or pursue a new challenge.

After eleven years at Sunoco, when I took stock, I knew that it was time to make a change. Even though I was happy and enjoyed my work and my colleagues very much, I could see that I had a choice to make: to stay in my comfort zone and watch ten years turn to twenty, or to step out of it to go for something new. Looking around, I was aware that those above me in the department still had many years of productive work ahead of them, enjoyed their work, and were good at it, so my opportunities to move up within the company were quite restricted. I asked myself, "Do I want to be born, live, and die in Philadelphia, or am I ready for a new challenge? What about my dream to live and work in Washington, DC?"

Those questions were largely rhetorical. As much as I loved Sunoco, I was ready for change, even though that change represented a certain level of risk (as change usually does). Although my decision to leave was relatively easy, finding the right opportunity again required that I take stock.

Even while at Sunoco, I had started to explore new interests. I had a lifelong interest in art and museums, and as I thought about personal gaps to fill outside the world of commercial law, I decided it was time to "fill a gap" by achieving qualifications in nonprofit management and art history. Since I already had a degree in business management, I surmised that pursuing further education in those two areas (in addition to my legal background) would make me a solid candidate for senior museum management, even though I had not been directly involved in the industry. I also shifted my volunteerism accordingly toward the arts and museum work.

After negotiating a four-week unpaid sabbatical from Sunoco to advance my art history and arts management studies, I spent a month in Europe with students from NYU learning the behind-the-scenes legal and business aspects of museum management, and as luck would have it, shortly after returning back home, I learned through networking at a cocktail party with a friend about a new museum of African American history soon to open in Detroit that was looking for a deputy director, and I applied for that position successfully.

Where would I be today if I had taken that road? I'll never know, because at the same time, I was also offered the role of deputy general counsel at ACC. It was a tough decision. I was faced with two attractive but very different options as I prepared to exit Sunoco.

Each option had its own set of risks and its own promise of opportunity ... which is why my second principle is Take Risk.

IN CHAPTER 2 YOU LEARNED:

- Take Stock involves taking an honest look at where you are, where you want to be, and what gaps you can see.
- Take Stock must become a regular habit (at least every six months) if you want to keep growing.
- The habit Take Stock is as essential for organizations as it is for individuals and is a habit that can also be applied to contexts outside of your career aspirations.
- Feedback from others is important when it comes to taking stock because you don't know what you don't know.
- Taking stock can be hard work, but that's not a good reason to neglect it.

Take Stock is such an essential step for making progress that I have developed a comprehensive checklist of qualifications and skills that you can use to guide your process. You may have your own items to add to the list, but this easy checklist will prompt your thinking and guide your timing and prioritization. Go to www.TakeSixHabits.com to download your checklist.

TAKE
SIX

CHAPTER THREE

TAKE RISK

I believe that one of life's greatest risks is never daring to risk.

—OPRAH WINFREY

"You can't do that, Jeanette!"

"You're too old to go to college …"

"No one in our family has ever done that!"

"Just be content looking after your family, and don't get ideas above yourself."

Jeanette was my godmother and my mother's best friend. She came from a large family, and despite having two hardworking parents, Jeanette and her siblings grew up very poor. She and my mother graduated from high school together, but being able to continue on to college was not possible for either Jeanette or my mother. Anxious to leave the family home and strike out on her own, Jeanette married

59

young and had two children, but her marriage did not last.

Divorced and with two daughters to care for, Jeanette worked hard to provide what they needed. But she also aspired to pursue higher education and become a teacher. So, while working full time to provide for herself and her daughters, who attended elite, top-ranked boarding schools, Jeanette enrolled in college in her forties despite not having been in a classroom for over twenty years. She managed to put herself through college and then go on to obtain her master's in education, in the face of protests from several of her family members and friends who sought to stifle her ambition and lower her sights. The criticism was hurtful, but Jeanette stuck to her guns. Her own daughters went on to college, too, and Jeanette fulfilled her dream of traveling, seeing the world, and exploring other cultures not just as a tourist, but by moving there as a resident, teacher, and expat.

The opposition Jeanette experienced when she was going to college and earning her teaching degree paled in comparison to the flak she experienced when she told people she had applied for a passport and was moving to Mexico to teach, but Jeanette was unflappable. She was curious about the world, was confident in her ability to learn new languages and navigate foreign cultures, loved teaching, and was willing to take risks and pursue her dreams. She was almost fifty when she first went overseas and spent most of the next twenty years exploring the world outside America, as she taught in Mexico, the US Virgin Islands, and the Middle East before moving back to the States and retiring. She made friends all over the world and impressed both her colleagues and students with her warmth and empowering example. Her visits to my childhood home to spend time with Mom were always exciting, as Jeanette told my sister and me stories about life overseas, the beauty of other cultures, the warmth she experienced from people in other countries, and their courage and commitment to their education. I know that her students, like my sister and me, took inspiration from her independent spirit, strong belief in herself, and ability to figure things out, take risks to pursue her dreams, and invest in her education.

> **I learned that there is no such thing as a ceiling for your dreams and that where you start does not limit where you end up, unless you let that happen to yourself.**

Whenever I think about my next step, my mind's eye sees my mother and godmother in front of me, and I can hear the echoes of their voices saying, "You can do it! I know you can." Jeanette knew how easy it is to get comfortable and stop striving for more, especially when you're afraid of seeming "above yourself." From her I learned that there is no such thing as a ceiling for your dreams and that where you start does not limit where you end up, unless you let that happen to yourself.

WHAT DOES TAKING RISK LOOK LIKE?

Everyone has their own level of tolerance for risk, but if you really want to find your place in the world, you need to dial up your risk tolerance regularly to ensure that you have a level of challenge that keeps you stretching for more. You don't necessarily need to move overseas, totally change direction, or even look for another position, but you need to remember that comfort and complacency are not compatible with growth and ambition.

I am fortunate to know a lot of amazing women, and the legendary Australian feminist icon Anne Summers is one of them. We were introduced through my sister, Vicki, who has been a dear friend of Anne and her husband, Chip, for several decades. As Anne said, "I developed an appetite for risk early in my life, once I realized that I would never be satisfied with the choices that life offered me." In the 1970s, Australian women were expected to marry, have children, and be economically dependent, and there were few "respectable" alternatives in conservative, monocultural Adelaide. She quickly learned that lowered expectations and restricted opportunities for girls were problems the world over and avidly devoured books containing the revolutionary ideas about women's liberation that were being published by American and British feminists.

Anne's landmark book, *Damned Whores and God's Police*, focused on both the role of women in the colonial period and in contemporary 1970s Australia.[5] It represented a massive reinterpretation of Australian history and the way in which Australians saw themselves. It tore down icons, challenged sacred cows, and attracted an enormous amount of attention—much of it hostile. Forty-six years later, this seminal book is still in print and has sold over 150,000 copies, and it has been updated several times to explain the evolution of society in response to the women's movement and the challenges that still exist. Not content with challenging the accepted historical narrative and overwhelming male dominance of contemporary society and culture, in 1986 Anne left a high-status permanent government job in Canberra to accept a position as a journalist and fulfill her longtime dream of living in New York. Even for someone as spirited and capable as Anne, it was a risky move.

The role didn't quite meet Anne's expectations, but it did create yet another opportunity: with her fellow-Australian business partner, Sandra Yates, who had come to New York to launch the

---

5   Anne Summers, *Damned Whores and God's Police: The Colonisation of Women in Australia*, 5th ed. (Sydney: NewSouth Publishing, 2016).

teenage magazine *Sassy*, she acquired the iconic feminist magazine *Ms.* (founded by Gloria Steinem). A few months later, they seized the opportunity of the magazine's being put up for sale by their Australian media company owner to undertake a management buyout of the company (only the second-ever women-led management buyout in US corporate history at that time) for $20 million! "People don't lend money to people who look like they need it," Sandra said, so they got themselves designer suits and headed for Wall Street, where they raised the money and signed the deal papers after an all-night closing session.

For a while they were the talk of the town. Everyone wanted to meet these two Australians who had raised all this money, started their own media company, and launched the hottest magazine in years. *Sassy* was an instant hit with both the thousands of teenage girls who read it and the advertisers who supported it. Anne reveled in every moment of her transformation from a lonely journalist on the fringe of New York society to the center of attention, but it didn't last. They were crushed by an advertiser boycott of *Sassy* that saw the publication lose $25 million projected advertising revenue in a single day. They were unable to service their huge debt and were finally forced to sell. Although their dream of becoming "media mogulettes in New York City" was crushed, Anne had no regrets then or later as she looked back. She soared, was excited by the great magazines they were producing, felt gratified by the reader response, and knew they were making a difference and leaving a historical mark. The experiences of those years will never leave her, nor did that failure diminish her appetite to take risks and see what she can make happen. Years later, following multiple awards, best-selling books, and accolades, including being named an "Australian legend" with her image emblazoned on a postage stamp, Anne continues to take risks and redefine herself, as it is now part of her DNA.

At the opposite end of the risk-taking spectrum is one of my former classmates, whom I'll call Alec. Alec is an accountant; he is hardworking, diligent, and cautious. He earned his degree and then his CPA, mastered his job, and worked his way up to middle management ... where he stayed year after year. He was a good, dependable worker, but after the first five years or so, there were no promotions, no expansions, and no movement. Class reunions must have been tough for Alec because people always asked if he'd been promoted, and time after time, he had to say, "No, but maybe next year." He stayed in that position for more than thirty years, most likely feeling underpaid, underchallenged, and passed over, but not willing to take the risk of looking for a new job in a different company. Eventually, he started his countdown to retirement—not because he was looking forward to his next stage of life, but just because he wanted to get away from his desk, his work, and his colleagues.

I understand Alec's desire for security and reluctance to do anything to compromise his ability to provide for his family, especially since he was just one generation removed from poverty, but I can't help wondering what he could have achieved if he had just stuck his neck out and taken some risk.

At some point, his stagnation meant that if he had ever needed to get a new job, he would have been an unappealing candidate. When most employers are interviewing prospects, they are looking for people whose backgrounds demonstrate that they are actively pursuing professional growth and are looking to acquire new skills and experience, because that suggests that they will bring energy and insight to their new position.

It would be wonderful to think that Alec was part of a small minority of people who get comfortable, avoid taking risks, and then become disengaged and simply go through the motions as they count down the years and months to retirement. Sadly, it can happen to anyone—even the most enthusiastic, ambitious, and motivated person—when they start to value security more than anything else.

My advice to my colleagues and mentees is that you should be developing new interests, pursuing education, and keeping your horizons open, even while you are happy in your current role. Risk-taking is a habit that needs to be exercised: if you're not in the habit of taking small risks regularly, then when opportunity arrives (and opportunity usually arrives hand in hand with risk), you may not be ready to step up and meet it.

As I look back on my own career, I see how the regular practice of taking risk sprang from my habit of taking stock and seeing the gaps that I needed to fill, as well as from being ready to stretch and grow. It was risky to

- accelerate my undergraduate degree so that I finished a year earlier than my cohort and was able to move on to law school, but I worked hard, balanced my social life, and maintained my GPA so that I could achieve that goal, even though many people were asking why I was in such a hurry;

- spend my summer working for free at Sunoco in the hope that my internship would help me gain experience I otherwise could not and get a position either there or at another top company;

- undertake education in an unrelated field (art history, nonprofit, and museum management) while I was practicing corporate law;

- ask for a four-week sabbatical while I was at Sunoco to go to

Europe to study museum management—at Sunoco, no one went away for four weeks, the only exception at that time being if a woman were pregnant and gave birth, she might take four weeks for maternity leave—clearly not a comparable "break";

- move from a higher-paying, safe, familiar position at Sunoco in my hometown to an organization in the nonprofit sector that was a fraction of the size and encompassed an entirely different set of responsibilities in a cliquish city like Washington, DC;

- volunteer to be ACC's representative to President Clinton's Lawyers for One America initiative—the mission of which was advancing diversity and pro bono service in the legal community; while I believed in the mission, I had no background in HR or diversity management—the only qualification that I had was that I was a "diverse lawyer" with lots of opinions and a willingness to read, study, and work hard so that I could contribute meaningfully; and

- leave my safe, stable position at ACC for the top job at MCCA, which was a much smaller organization and, frankly, too broke to meet payroll. I'd been warned about jumping too quickly, but I was humiliated to discover that as a corporate lawyer who handled due diligence and looked into the creditworthiness and financial soundness of companies to merge or acquire, I had completely failed to look closely before I leaped. Once I discovered the situation (on my first day!), I realized that if I did not turn the organization around and if it failed on my watch, my reputation would suffer, not that of the charismatic founder from whom I inherited the organization.

All of these risks paid off (with the aid of large doses of strategic planning, hard work, faith, and, yes, sometimes prayer), but there was no guarantee of success when I stepped out each time.

SUCCESS LIES AT THE INTERSECTION OF RISK AND OPPORTUNITY (IF YOU'VE PREPARED)

Risk doesn't always mean moving to an entirely different place; it can be just as risky to stay where you are and accept stretch assignments or lead a project unlike any you've experienced previously. When you choose to develop new skills or explore facets of your work more deeply, as I did when I undertook studies in nonprofit museum management and art history, you expose yourself to risk. Maybe other people will see your initiative as a threat, or (like my godmother, Jeanette, and friend Anne) you may discover a new path and feel compelled to follow it in the face of opposition.

Looking back on history, I think that there are periods when large portions of the population are strongly tempted to become complacent and risk averse because life is so safe, comfortable, and predictable. As a racial minority, I wasn't as well cocooned, connected, or safe as others may have been, so I felt I had no choice but to take bigger risks. However, I have noticed that among my female, racial or cultural minority, or LGBTQ+ colleagues, some appear to have a sense of "I've made it this far, I am doing well, and it's OK to stop here and just maintain." Social and technological disruption has blasted through that sense of predictability for now, which may prove a good thing, even if it creates tough choices, but it's up to you to develop the risk-taking skills to thrive in a rapidly changing world.

One of the findings that emerged from research during my years at MCCA that focused specifically on women's opportunities and progress in law was that women are generally less inclined to step out and take the kinds of risks that provide momentum for their careers or expand their horizons. A recent study about women, leadership, and keys to professional success confirms that little has changed over the past ten-plus years and that while the majority of women believe that "people who take more career risks progress more quickly than others," only 43 percent of women were prepared to act on that belief, with many preferring to play it safe, rather than playing to win.[6] Other research suggests that tolerance for seeing risks as opportunities rather than threats is tied to perceptions regarding self-confidence and belief in our own competence, which would suggest that the first three of my six recommended essential habits can play an important role in your progress and growth.[7] First, Take Stock requires you to measure the gap between where you are and where you want to go, and if you consistently discover that you have no gap, then you know that you need to expand your goals. Second, Take Risk entails building the habit of taking consistent, calculated risks, which helps us develop a growth mindset and insatiable curiosity that pays off in many areas of life in addition to accelerating our careers and helping us achieve our goals. Third, Take Credit (which is the subject of the next chapter) encourages you to regularly inventory your accomplishments and contributions, which builds self-confidence.

The evolution of these notions into actual habits underlies a pivotal realization that has influenced how I advise and challenge

---

6   KPMG Women's Leadership Study, *Risk, Resilience, Reward: Mastering the three R's is the key to women's success in the workplace* (KPMG, 2019).

7   Norris Krueger Jr. and Peter R. Dickson, "How Believing in Ourselves Increases Risk Taking: Perceived Self-Efficacy and Opportunity Recognition," *Decision Sciences* 25, no. 3 (May 1994): 385-400.

people who ask me for help. I always knew that I would have to make a habit of stepping out of my comfort zone if I wanted to achieve my goals, but I somehow overlooked the reality that other people also needed to do this. These studies helped me see that taking risk is a universal principle of success. Playing it safe and refusing to bet on yourself often leads to regrets and lost opportunities. As a woman of color in an industry dominated by people who don't look like me, I worked hard to excel and to fill every possible gap in my knowledge and experience, despite sometimes feeling tempted to hold on to the familiar achievements I had already gained. Staying at organizations with managers who already knew my strengths and appreciated my contributions would have been easier than moving forward and forging new paths. Hunkering down in roles that I had already mastered would have been safer than stepping out and risking failure. Equally, they would have stifled my growth.

Over the years, as I have had opportunities to talk with corporate leaders about the success gap, it became clear that one of the characteristics of highly successful people in any field is their willingness to step out of their comfort zone and stretch themselves by taking calculated risks based on their values and belief in themselves. I was fortunate to be able to interview Ken Frazier, retired CEO of Merck & Co., who put it succinctly in the context of his own experience: "I always felt that I was willing to step into a void, to take a risk despite any uncertainty or unpopularity surrounding that void. I use my values to guide my decisions ... Of course, I feel anxiety, but I never let it stop me. You either step into that void or you don't." As Ken says, the essence of leadership is a willingness to step up to fill a void. Sometimes that may require taking on a tough assignment or project that is riddled with challenges and problems to be solved in order to turn a bad situation around. Other times it may require taking a coura-geous, principled, and potentially unpopular stand and living with the anxiety and uncertainty that will bring, and we'll explore the habit of Take a Stand in a future chapter.

Let's explore the concept of Take Risk in the context of applying for a new job, especially one that's a level or two above a current role. A study on the impact of workplace risk-taking and career prospects suggests that employers look favorably on candidates who have a history of risk-taking and that even failure does not cause significant harm to their prospects.[8] If you are wondering whether an unsuc-cessful attempt to compete for a role will hurt your chances, this data should encourage you to go ahead and put your name forward.

One of the things I've noticed in candidate assessment is that if there are ten key criteria, you will invariably get applications from candidates who meet only three or four of those criteria, yet who confidently assert their qualifications and preparedness in their cover letters and interviews, whereas other candidates who may meet seven or eight of the criteria are apologetic and hesitant because they focus on the perceived gap in not having all ten criteria rather than their multiple strengths. More often than not, it was the men who applied knowing they met three of ten qualifications and women who felt reluctant to apply because they met only seven of the ten. When you are looking at roles that will extend your expertise and for which you may feel unqualified, it's important to Take Stock—so you can decide whether this is a risk that is aligned with your overall goals for your career. The path that you have in front of you is often a far better guide than the job description and criteria set out by the company.

---

8   S. R. Fisk and J. Overton, "Bold or Reckless? The Impact of Workplace Risk-Taking on Attributions and Expected Outcomes," *PLOS One* 15, no. 3 (2020), https://journals. plos.org/plosone/article?id=10.1371/journal.pone.0228672.

Here are some useful questions that will help you decide whether to apply for that stretch position or whether to stay where you are and keep looking around:

- Will this role enable you to develop or consolidate key skills that align with your bigger career and life goals?

- Will this role provide you with opportunities to develop new relationships that may stand you in good stead in the future?

- Is this role a stepping-stone to your next goal, or is it just a flattering distraction?

- Does the company culture sound like a good fit, and do employees tend to stay at the company?

- Does this feel like a stretch opportunity or an impossible challenge?

- Have you asked all the questions you need to about the role and the company, and do you feel as though you have received honest answers?

Failure is not the end of the world—unless you choose to turn it into that—and if that is your attitude, you will never achieve all that you could. This is why it's so very important to practice taking risks, both large and small, early and often so that you develop a stronger tolerance for risk.

SELF-LIMITATION IS OFTEN THE GREATEST HINDRANCE TO ADVANCEMENT

If you think back to some of the stories that I've already shared, you will see a pattern of self-limitation that had to be overcome. Jen lacked confidence that she could speak in front of people, and she would never have put herself forward to do so; a little push in the right direction enabled her to grow. Every day during my first summer at Sunoco, I walked into reception and made my way to the legal department certain that I would fall short, even though I was giving it everything I had. We were both wrong to limit how we saw ourselves.

In chapter 2, I talked about taking stock, identifying the gaps you need to fill, and eliminating those gaps. Taking risks is about having confidence in your ability to fill those gaps and solve those problems so that you are willing to put yourself forward rather than keeping your head down. It's about recognizing that those gaps don't necessarily disqualify you from seeking and achieving advancement. The next chapter, "Take Credit," is about regularly tracking your accomplishments so that you can take pride in them and create awareness in those around you. Most job listings are a wish list to some degree. In addition to the specific criteria that must be met (e.g., law degree, bar admission), there are also elastic expectations, such as years of experience and soft skills. I have rarely come across a candidate who met every criterion on the list, and the best-qualified candidates are usually aware of the fact that a position is going to challenge them and provide opportunities to grow and learn new skills.

Successful people, in any field, are those who are willing to face challenges, secure in their proven track record for figuring things out, even if the path to success involves failure and mistakes. If you're afraid to make mistakes, then you're probably taking yourself far too seriously, as I used to do. So stop trying to be perfect, and loosen up!

Ann Mulé, one of my Sunoco heroes, used to tell me to lighten up from time to time, and she set an example. She took her work and responsibilities seriously but used laughter to help us keep everything in perspective. A sense of humor when it comes to yourself, your achievements, skills, and failures removes a lot of pressure and opens up new horizons. It's probably an essential skill for long-term success because it not only helps you to be more relatable, but it also defuses situations in which there might otherwise be a tendency to blame others when you encounter problems, and humor can be used to encourage people when they fail as well.

CALCULATED RISKS VERSUS LEAPS OF FAITH ... WHAT IS THE DIFFERENCE?

When I left Sunoco and joined ACC, I abandoned a successful corporation with a workforce of more than thirty thousand employees, where I was doing well, and I took a significant pay cut to be part of a bar association with about thirty staff. There were plenty of people who fully expected that I'd use my option to return to Sunoco before the two years were up, acknowledging my mistake. Some of my friends thought I was crazy, knowing how hard and long I had pursued that long-standing dream of becoming the corporate lawyer at the *Fortune* 500 company.

I saw it from a different angle. For me, it was a calculated risk. I had already achieved my career goal of becoming a corporate counsel, and it was time to set new goals, grow in new areas, and make a life for myself outside my native Philadelphia. This was a move that would enable me to develop new entrepreneurial skills, become more self-sufficient, manage people and budgets, and gain familiarity with a range of business and administrative issues from which I was always insulated by the sheer size of Sunoco. During my regular process of taking stock of where I was, I had identified a growing sense of complacency. My work had become predictable, the career ladder was crowded at the upper rungs, and I had mastered the skills I needed to resolve problems successfully. It was time to set new goals and new challenges that would keep me learning and push me out of my comfort zone. I knew that with my background as in-house counsel at a *Fortune* 500 company, I would be able to offer insights into ways that our bar association could better serve its members. So I knew that it was my time to experience something new, despite the inherent risks.

In 2000, when I was evaluating the offer from MCCA, I also took a calculated risk in deciding to leave ACC, where I had established credibility and influence. Actually, I thought I was taking a calculated risk, but it was actually more like a leap of faith because I made the mistake of failing to do proper financial due diligence. When I realized that I had moved from a financially sound organization to one drowning in debt and looked at the magnitude of the turnaround I would have to lead, I was angry at myself for my negligence. I felt stupid; I was ashamed of myself, and there were days when, even with our line of credit from the bank, the only thing I could do was kneel down and pray that we would get enough donor checks to make payroll and cover our bills. The only thing that stopped me from going back to ACC and asking for my old job was pride, as well as a burning commitment to MCCA's mission to advance diversity and bring down some of the barriers that prevent underrepresented groups from advancing.

It worked out all right in the end, and looking back, I'm grateful for the experience, relationships, and confidence that my dramatic turnaround of a debt-laden nonprofit gave me, but I wouldn't recommend it as a general practice. On my worst days, I could comfort myself with the fact that if I did fail to turn MCCA around, I would have given it everything I had, and no one who knew the circumstances could have blamed me for the failure. I won't ever omit again the step of investigating the finances of an organization prior to taking a management role, but I am still grateful for the experience, and it demonstrates that even when you think you know everything, there is always an element of uncertainty in life unless you are content with mediocrity. When you Take Risk, it is a bit like that: you can't run two tracks in parallel; you can only make choices and learn resilience and wisdom from them.

WHEN IS IT TIME TO TAKE RISK?

Life is an inherently risky and uncertain journey, especially if your goal is to cram as much growth, vibrancy, and experience into every day as possible. So the answer to "When should I take risks?" is really "Every day."

My dear friend Crystal is beautiful and brilliant. She is African American and single and has a distinguished reputation as a specialist in both trademark and commercial law. A few years ago, she was tapped by the management of her corporate law department to leave her familiar home and work environment in the United States and challenge herself both personally and professionally by moving to Dubai, UAE, to work as the lead lawyer for one of her company's divisions. Moving to the Middle East had never been anything she had contemplated and likely was not on her "bucket list" to do. So it was not without a lot of soul searching and taking stock that she agreed to step out of her comfort zone and Take a Risk to accept a role unlike any she had previously taken on.

In addition to moving to Dubai, which entailed a major cultural shift as well as leaving her friends and family, she was also given very challenging growth targets and goals to meet in her new role as a generalist lawyer responsible for issues ranging from data privacy, employment, contract negotiation, transportation of construction equipment, supply and parts issues, disputes, and so on. Crystal was willing to leave her existing position, move to a new country, develop new relationships, expand her skills, and take frontline responsibility for legal issues without any guarantee of success because she knew that the move would propel her career forward unless, of course, she messed up badly. Of course, she didn't. In fact, she received high praise from all who worked with her at that business unit. At the end of her time in Dubai, she was asked to return to the States, take a senior legal role at the corporate headquarters, and within months of returning was appointed by the general counsel to serve on the law department's management committee. Her appointment marked the first time for a person of color to be invited to take a seat at that particular table, and I believe that is something that likely would not have happened had Crystal not stepped out of her comfort zone, taken some major risks, and proven her worth.

When Crystal called me from time to time from Dubai, I knew I was going to enjoy the conversation and hear a new perspective on life. From her experiences finding a place to live and a new hair stylist, to her shopping adventures and experiences with local customs, there was plenty for her to learn and share, but most of all, I could see how much her insight and curiosity had grown in the midst of taking on a new professional challenge.

Any move or change carries a degree of risk, but there's an even greater risk in sitting where you are: the risk of stagnation. Even without the dire financial straits that MCCA was experiencing, the move from ACC would still have been risky at a professional level. I was moving from a reputable bar association where the top tier of the corporate counsel sector came for education, networking, and professional services to a relatively little-known organization with a mission to promote diversity in that most homogenous profession: law. However, I was also stepping up to the challenge of a new level of organizational leadership and furthering a cause to which I was (and remain) deeply committed.

Once again, the essential habits Take Stock and Take Risk were closely intertwined. As I met with the accountants and the board of directors over those first few days and weeks, we were balancing the vision of where we wanted to be with the magnitude of the gap we were facing. It was clear that we couldn't close that gap without taking risk, but the question in all of their minds was, "Can she close that large a gap?" Our gross receipts for the previous year were under $1 million, and we were almost $900,000 in debt. The bank had (reluctantly) given us additional credit, but the board members were going to have to cut some checks and support serious fundraising efforts if we were to honor our obligations. Business as usual certainly wouldn't solve our problems. On the other hand ... I looked at that list of our members. I thought about our vision and mission. And I made the decision on my own, without asking the board, to expand MCCA's mission to be broader than just women and racial or ethnic minorities. MCCA needed a bigger tent and much wider appeal. So I risked moving MCCA's advocacy in ways that were not yet widely adopted in the legal profession to include sexual orientation and gender identity, disability status, and generational differences.

Our whole team worked together furiously to plan and execute MCCA's major fundraising awards dinner for our members in New York that fall. Over the next eighteen months, we repaid all our creditors, and by the time I left MCCA ten years later, we had grown to an annual budget of $4.5 million with almost as much in investment reserves. Every member of the team had developed new skills and thrived on all that risk-induced innovation. Looking back, despite the stress (which I don't miss), I see it as one of the most dramatic periods of personal growth that took the confidence I had gained from past risk-taking to a whole new level. As a result, I am a more confident and capable leader, and the risks I've taken over the years have been fundamental to my success.

EVALUATING RISKS: THE PROCESS

Planning and evaluating risk are closely tied to the process of closing the gap between where you are and where you want to be. When I decided that I needed to learn how to network and carry on a professional conversation, I had to Take a Risk and actually go to the Baltimore Convention Center and talk to people in pursuit of my goal. The first time I was asked to chair an event on behalf of Sunoco, it was a step on the path to comfort being in charge. The important thing here isn't the **size** of the risk; it's your willingness to have courage, step out of your comfort zone over and over again, and suspend self-criticism and self-doubt over the fear that you will choke or fail. It's also your readiness to get up and take another risk, even when you fail, secure in the knowledge that your failures don't define you unless you choose to let them do so.

Here are three key questions you should keep in mind when considering whether to Take a Risk in a specific context or not:

1. How will this help me develop the habit of stepping out of my comfort zone and taking on challenges for which I do not feel fully prepared so that I can develop self-confidence and skills for the future?

2. Even if I were to fail at this, would I learn valuable lessons and acquire valuable experience?

3. How will this help me expand or develop my network of supporters and people who can vouch for my tenacity and growth mindset?

Hopefully, you will not use this process to reject all risk and decide that you're "not good" at X. My mother's belief in my ability to succeed was a big factor in my risk tolerance. I always knew that the only thing that would really disappoint her was if I didn't strive for things that I wanted and that her response to failure would be to examine the situation and discover what went wrong so that I could learn from it, but it's not merely a question of upbringing. There are so many people who start out full of ambition but then experience an obstacle or challenge and, as a consequence, decide to withdraw, abandon their aspirations, and play it safe. There are also others who start their careers with their heads down, working hard, determined not to make themselves conspicuous, afraid of making mistakes, failing, or admitting weakness, who ultimately decide that they need to Take Risk to support causes they believe in or reach a bit beyond their grasp, and who develop a stronger risk tolerance later in life.

When Robin, a twenty-year veteran in ACC's Washington, DC, office, agreed to relocate to London to take on a new senior-level assignment, she faced multiple levels of risk. She was leaving a position that she enjoyed and excelled at and passing on her responsibilities to another colleague, so there was no turning back to her former position. She was also moving to a new country where she would have to make a new home, adjust to new customs, and navigate new relationships to build a local support base since the move would disrupt existing relationships with friends and family who were now miles and time zones away.

For Robin, the move was a calculated risk and was well timed. Her youngest child would be starting college; there was a degree of security since she was familiar with ACC and had professional relationships with many people in the UK and Europe, so she could draw on the skills, relationships, and abilities she had honed over two decades working with the association's membership. Plus, she was excited at the prospect of living and working in London. As she evaluated the opportunity, she measured the gains against the risks and then accepted the offer, trusting herself to successfully navigate the inevitable challenges, even though she could not predict exactly what the outcome would be. After more than a year in the new role, Robin has made great strides and strengthened key relationships in the region as well as demonstrated her ability to adapt and take on new challenges.

TRUSTED ADVISORS, NAYSAYERS, AND RISK

The only person you absolutely must have in your court when you make a risky move is yourself. If you can't back yourself to give that risky effort everything you have, then you probably shouldn't make the move. This is why, even though Take Stock and Take Risk are separate, they're also closely intertwined. It's imperative to Take Stock before you Take Risk so that you are aware of your strengths as well as your weaknesses and won't get mired down by the things you lack.

Even though **you** are the key stakeholder and decision maker in your life's adventures, it's important to build and maintain a network of trusted advisors who will help you evaluate options, because we all have blind spots. We'll discuss the importance of this more in chapter 5 where we talk about the habit of Take a Hand, but when it comes to Take Risk, it's important to assess the risk-tolerance levels and risk profiles of your advisors and factor that into your thinking.

The only person you absolutely must have in your court when you make a risky move is yourself.

A young man named Andrew discovered this firsthand. Both his parents are successful professionals, and he received an excellent private school education and then started college. At the end of his first year, he decided to quit and went home to tell his parents that college wasn't for him. His father went ballistic when he realized that his only son wasn't even going to finish two years of college and earn an associate degree!

Andrew was fortunate that his mother supported him and pointed out that if college wasn't for him, that was fine, but he needed to earn a livelihood, and she was persuasive in getting Andrew's father to come around to that view. His mother helped Andrew sift through his options, and he chose to pursue a trade and become an electrician. Now Andrew has successfully completed his training, gained experience, and set his sights on specializing in home theater and sound installation with a goal to own his own business one day.

It took a lot of courage to go home to his parents, tell them that he was quitting school, and listen to accusations that he was "throwing away his future." It also took courage to choose a job that involves manual labor rather than the white-collar work he had been brought up to value, but Andrew was willing to take the risk and humble enough to realize that his parents were right when they told him that he needed to pursue some kind of training.

In the same way, when I told the guidance counselor about my desire to accelerate my degree, I was put firmly in my place. She probably thought that was the end of the story, but for me, it was only the beginning. Jeanette had a similar experience when she wanted to study and become a teacher in her forties and then, in her fifties, work overseas. Many people told her that she couldn't fulfill her dreams and thought the subject was closed. It wasn't. The same was true of Anne and Crystal, as they stepped out of the familiar to pursue new opportunities. We all kept asking questions, looking for other people who were doing what we wanted to do, or would at least offer support to help us plan and work toward our goals. Along the way, we each developed a trusted network of advisors to whom we could turn for help. You will need to build your own network too.

Over the years, I've built up a strong "cabinet" of advisors to whom I can go with a plan, a dream, or a problem. All of these people understand the importance of strategic risk-taking, and they're willing to be brutally honest when that is required. I started out with a small support base, and it has grown over the years, as I carefully nurtured relationships and planned how to stay in touch with people (as I'll discuss in chapter 5, where we talk about the essential habit Take a Hand). Hopefully, among that group you'll hear a variety of opinions about most of the risks you're considering, and you'll feel a sense of support for your decision as well as receive some honest feedback about your preparedness.

There are some risks that will not end well for you. When that is the case, you need to recognize that and, depending on the situation, either move on or stay away. If you're in an environment where you look around you and don't see anyone who looks like you, supports you, or relates to you, and you don't have the internal or external support you need to soldier through, then do not feel you must be stoic—it's time to move on.

RISKS, MISTAKES, AND FAILURE

In today's world, it seems as though we're focused on the appearance of perfection and success to the detriment of growth and development. One of the reasons I hesitated before writing this book is that I was afraid that focusing on the positive habits I've developed would make me sound as though I have everything together. Hopefully, you've already realized that that isn't the whole story. Behind each of these lessons are plenty of stumbles and failures. You can't grow to your fullest potential without them.

When I think back on the many inspiring people whom I have had the privilege of meeting and working with over the years, one of the things I've noticed is their willingness to risk failure ... often very visible failure, like the willingness to run for political office and take the risk of having your past dissected for all to see and your success or failure a matter of public record. It's the price you pay for being willing to step forward and lead. If you are risk averse in your investments, that's fine, and your returns may prove modest but acceptable. However, if you are risk averse in your approach to your career, chances are you'll end up stagnating and losing out on multiple opportunities.

If you are risk averse in your approach to your career, chances are you'll end up stagnating and losing out on multiple opportunities.

One of my fellow legal colleagues fell into this trap. After all the work she put into completing her degree, finding a position with a top law firm, and gaining experience and respect, she fell into the "good enough" trap. Around the five- to ten-year mark, she started to avoid challenges and stick with things that were familiar and comfortable. Don't get me wrong—she was a great colleague and did an excellent job for her clients, but she lost the bright edginess that made her stand out and ultimately looked to put in her time, waiting for retirement. She was happy enough, comfortable enough, valued enough ... and that "enough" has been a warning to me to make sure that I Take Risk and challenge myself. Maybe it's not the way everyone wants to live, but I'm keen to immerse myself in life's possibilities and keep striving rather than to sit still and enjoy "just enough."

Risk and mistakes go hand in hand, so if you are going to take risks, you will need to be prepared to own and take responsibility when you make a mistake. Early in my career, I realized that the way managers treated mistakes and failures had two immediate consequences:

1. They affected team members' willingness to take risks and solve problems effectively in the future.

2. They affected how long people stayed in a position.

There were some managers who were so negative when mistakes were made that everyone was desperate to hide them and often prone to point fingers of blame in the wrong direction. This often meant that you couldn't address the problem until it had grown out of all proportion. It also meant that people were sometimes too frightened of making a mistake to take the initiative.

We all make mistakes sometimes. That's part of being human. I learned from seeing what happened when mistakes were treated like mortal sins that could never be redeemed or recovered from that there were better ways to handle it. Fortunately, I also had plenty of great examples, and now I make sure that everyone working with me understands the appropriate process for handling mistakes. It's part of leadership expectations.

Here's how we handle mistakes:

1. Take ownership and call it out yourself. Don't wait for it to be discovered. Don't try to blame someone else.

2. Apologize for the role you played in creating a problem, causing disruption, or contributing to whatever negativity was caused by the mistake.

3. Ask yourself, "Is there a way to solve or undo this mistake, and minimize the damage or expense?"

4. If there is, follow through and correct the mistake, and minimize the damage or expenses.

5. Then shake it off and move on. You cannot dwell on your mistakes or beat yourself up.

When you handle mistakes this way, it may seem as though you are taking a risk, but really you boost your own self-respect and confidence, and you also establish a reputation for reliability and trustworthiness with your colleagues. They have confidence that you are willing to call out your own mistakes and take responsibility for setting them right to the extent possible.

Yes, Take Risk can lead to mistakes and failures. They can be mistakes of judgment or of execution. It's only when you are willing to stand up and own those mistakes rather than shifting the blame onto others that you are in a position to Take Credit for your successes, which is the subject of the next chapter.

IN CHAPTER 3 YOU LEARNED:

As a key habit, Take Risk is an essential part of staying engaged in your life and work.

- If you can create a safety net to fall back on, that will make taking risk easier.
- Risk-taking is a muscle you build through practice; you can start with small risks and then move on to larger ones.
- Don't take yourself too seriously; no one else does or should.
- Do your due diligence thoroughly so that you are not surprised by the magnitude of the risks you are facing.
- Sharing risks and being supported by people in your network build trust within your relationships.

TAKE SIX

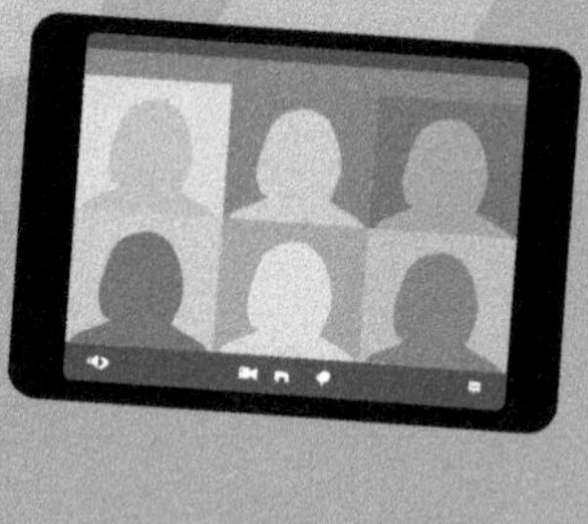

CHAPTER FOUR

TAKE CREDIT

The real difficulty is to overcome how you think about yourself.

—MAYA ANGELOU

You've probably met someone like Jack, a former colleague of mine, who is a master at taking credit and attracting the spotlight. Some people would get irritated by Jack's apparently endless ability to create a positive impression and help people realize the value he brings to his team and the company, but I prefer to view him as a model whose example we can all learn and draw lessons from. At company social events, Jack makes a point of talking to a variety of people and asks insightful and strategic questions about the projects on which they are working. Whether he is talking to the newest hire or senior management, he demonstrates that he isn't looking at projects or assignments as discrete elements but that he is considering how they contribute to the company's overarching goals and mission. As a result, he leaves a strong impression of accomplishment with people at every level. In meetings, Jack doesn't just talk about the items he has completed or is working on, but he also manages to strategically tie them into the bigger picture so that when he asks for assistance, other members of the team can easily see what is needed and understand the level of strategic, bigger-picture significance the project has. By tying his contributions to team and company-wide goals, Jack makes a significant impression on those in management, and as a result, his rapid rise through the ranks was assured—as was the jealousy of some of his less vocal and strategic colleagues.

One of Jack's coworkers, whom I'll call Sheila, started working at the company about the same time as Jack. Sheila was diligent, disciplined, and hardworking. If you wanted someone on your team who would make sure that the job was completed on time, to specifications, and without fuss, Sheila was the person you would choose for the job. She would show up, give the task everything she had, and quietly take up the slack for others without drawing any attention to her sacrifices and efforts. Her teammates relied on her expertise and dependability heavily, but somehow, they never talked about her much, and she kept her head down and got on with the work, so while Jack was fast-tracked for promotion again and again, Sheila stayed on a steady path of promotion by seniority. Managers would say, "Sheila loves her work and just wants to get on with doing it. She doesn't like the limelight." And they would pass over her for special opportunities because she was such a valuable backstop. Jack liked Sheila, and he really appreciated her thoroughness and insight when they worked on projects together, so he tried to give her some tips on how to Take Credit for her contributions, but Sheila wouldn't listen. She was waiting for others to notice her accomplishments and reward what she saw as her substantial value.

At first, Sheila was happy to work hard and contribute wholeheartedly without much acclaim because she fully expected that she would reap the rewards for the contributions that everyone acknowledged and then quickly forgot. Time passed, and little recognition came. Sheila kept doing good work. Her managers kept on being grateful for her thoroughness, commitment, and expertise, but still she was just a cog in the wheel, coming to work and dependably doing her job. Over time, she became angry and bitter about her lack of recognition, especially as she watched Jack's rise. The quality of her work remained high, but when she talked about her colleagues, she would often bad-mouth them—especially Jack—and complain privately about how they had taken advantage of her to get ahead. Gradually, people stopped selecting her on collaborative projects and avoided her as much as possible because she went into every project with the assumption that she would do most of the work and others would take the credit for it. Eventually, she left the job, and her coworkers were not sorry to see her go.

Admittedly, Sheila's managers might have done a better job. But Sheila's biggest problem was that she never learned how to present herself in a strong and credible way and to Take Credit for her own successes graciously. She kept waiting for others to recognize her without doing or saying any of the things that would have made her more visible and her contributions more memorable. Worse still, Jack's kind offers to help were rebuked because Sheila was too proud and resentful of Jack's success. If you are reading this and want to learn how not to be a "Sheila," read on.

THE IMPORTANCE OF LEARNING HOW TO TAKE CREDIT

Imagine a busy executive, who is working long days and carrying a heavy burden of responsibility. She has a vacancy to fill and decides to promote someone within the department. Maybe she asks her managers to put forward some names, but they're all busy too. The chances are that the opportunity will be given to people who are good at self-promotion because they will be the names that spring to mind first.

When you develop the habit of taking credit for what you do, you make it easy for other people to remember and reward your achievements and recognize the ways in which your work contributes to overall goals and objectives.

Is that fair? Maybe not, but it's the reality that you need to deal with, so in this chapter we'll talk about how you can learn to Take Credit gracefully and reap the powerful benefits of recognition, so you don't end up being passed over like Sheila.

Careers and opportunities are built on track records and performance. When you develop the habit of taking credit for what you do, you make it easy for other people to remember and reward your achievements and recognize the ways in which your work contributes to overall goals and objectives. If you are going to Take Credit effectively, then you need to

1. track your own accomplishments and contributions;

2. understand clearly how those tasks and projects contribute to your company's strategies;

3. identify the dangers that you averted or avoided and the expenses that you saved;

4. document your progress in HR records that are reflected in your personnel file; and

5. learn how to effectively talk to others about your contribution and share the impact you made.

If your goal is to rise through the ranks and make a difference, then these are important skills to develop, and Take Credit is an essential habit. People (especially busy people) have short memories when it comes to who contributed to what outcome and to what extent they did so. The idea of the unsung hero sounds noble, but the results can be devastating both personally and professionally, and they also deprive organizations of talent.

TRACK YOUR OWN ACCOMPLISHMENTS

Many people wrongly assume that those around them will notice their efforts and contributions, remember them, and ensure they get the recognition they deserve. The reality is that everyone around you is focused on their own work and career, absorbed in completing projects, reaching goals that keep them on track, and looking for ways to make their work easier. Therefore, it is your responsibility to keep track of your projects and accomplishments.

Memory is actually very easily influenced and modified. In a study on memory retrieval, cognitive neurologist Donna Bridge confirmed the results of previous studies that demonstrate the extent to which inaccurate memory retrieval has long-term effects on the recall of specific memories. As she put it, "A memory is not simply an image produced by time traveling back to the original event—it can be an image that is somewhat distorted because of the prior times you remembered it."[9] In the context of taking credit, there are two applications of this.

1. *It is important to document your accomplishments regularly because the longer the interval between the action and the reflection on that action, the more you are likely to forget.*

An accomplishment is anything that you do in the course of your work that contributes to the successful fulfillment of your organization's mission. It includes projects you work on, certifications or courses you complete, introductions you are able to make, mistakes you are able to identify or fix, problems you are able solve, costs you figure out how to save, people you are able to help, new skills that you acquire through training ... the list is practically endless.

Do not confuse hours worked with impact achieved. Time spent does not necessarily translate to results accomplished.

At most law firms, people are required to track their time daily so they can determine how many hours they need to charge the client. This is a very valuable source of information when it comes to tracking your time, but it may not be the best for tracking your accomplishments. One insignificant matter may take a lot of time to complete, but a noteworthy contribution or accomplishment may have been completed relatively quickly. It is worth underscoring this point—do not confuse hours worked with impact achieved. Time spent does not necessarily translate to results accomplished. That is why you should develop the weekly (at

---

9   Donna J. Bridge and Ken A. Paller, "Neural Correlates of Reactivation and Retrieval-Induced Distortion," *Journal of Neuroscience* 32, no. 35 (2012), 12144-51.

worst, monthly) habit of creating a private record of achievements as well as your other contributions to the achievements of a group or a significant project. Whenever you walk out of a meeting and think, "I did a great job identifying that potential problem so that we could discuss a solution," or something similar, you should make a note of it as soon as possible. By Friday, you will probably have forgotten all about it, and then, in three weeks' time when someone explains how implementing the solution early saved thousands of dollars, you will have forgotten. I know you are busy getting things done, but you can get an app on your phone and quickly dictate your notes in just a few moments. That way you'll keep a running personal record of your contributions, independent of anything that your company holds.

In addition to providing you with substantive data to present to others during performance reviews, job interviews, and when you may be asking for new opportunities, this record also provides you with an objective list that you can use to bolster your own confidence. It is easy to get so busy and worn out that you look back on your week and think, "What did I actually **accomplish**?"

2. *Two people rarely perceive or interpret the same situation in the identical way, and the passing of time makes that difference even greater.*

This has several implications, but it makes it even more important that you document things as soon as possible after the fact. Your colleagues may later remember the situation differently, and you will be tempted to believe that your memory is playing tricks, which undermines your confidence. Eyewitnesses to an accident or other incident frequently have completely different stories to tell, and that is equally true when it comes to projects, meetings, and other workplace affairs.[10] When Jack made a point of interacting with senior management at social events and spoke with insight and excitement about things that drove the company's success, executives received an impression that subsequent encounters with him reinforced.

UNDERSTAND YOUR CONTRIBUTION TO THE COMPANY'S MISSION

Fast-track careers aren't just built on your ability to execute tasks and meet targets. They're also built on an understanding of the context in which those tasks are being performed and their strategic roles in the company.

As you document your accomplishments, you should also think about what that does and where it fits in the bigger plan. Think of these accomplishments as a "what-which" statement. Here are some examples:

- I identified and corrected a calculation error in the budget, which reduced our profits and meant that our department needed to reconsider our expenditures.

- I completed my CPA, which means that if I were to look for a new position, I could ask for a higher base salary.

- I managed a social media strategy, which resulted in 20 percent higher sales volume from the target market.

By putting your accomplishments in perspective for your own

---

10   Hal Arkowitz and Scott O. Lilienfield, "Why Science Tells Us Not to Rely on Eyewitness Accounts," *Scientific American*, January 1, 2010, https://www.scientificamerican.com/article/do-the-eyes-have-it/.

benefit, you'll find that you are able to raise these points more easily when you're talking to others. As a consequence, you'll not only build a reputation that is highly sought after in management, but you will also increase your skill in this area.

IDENTIFY THE DAMAGE THAT YOU AVERTED

Sometimes the actions you didn't take are just as crucial as the ones you did. Mistakes are often costly to rectify. Once, a significant error was made in a magazine insert that the company I worked for published regularly. We did not realize the error until it had been printed and the magazines were ready for distribution. Fortunately, we were valued customers, and when I called to ask the distributor to delay the mailing while the error was corrected and the insert reprinted, the request was favorably received. If we had more carefully proofread that piece, we could have saved a lot of time, money, and stress! However, I took ownership of the mistake as soon as I spotted it and took the appropriate action to set things right.

I'm not suggesting that you write down every time you catch a typo—the internet is a lot more forgiving and easily revised than print, anyway—but do keep track of those times when the questions you raised, mistakes you identified, information you offered, or alternative pathways you suggested made a difference. It probably happens more often than you remember.

Some time ago, our IT department made the decision to move our association's data storage and backup systems from physical servers to the cloud. That was a strategic move intended to save money and time (which it did), but the conversion process was intensive, and some people questioned whether it was worthwhile. No one could have anticipated that their decision and forethought would make such a dramatic difference until our entire team had to cease in-office work and quickly pivot to working remotely from home. Without those earlier good judgment calls, our team would have taken far longer to transition to an unanticipated remote work model. These are the types of decisions that should be carefully recorded as contributions.

DOCUMENT YOUR PROGRESS IN HR RECORDS

In addition to your ongoing personal tracking of accomplishments, you should make every effort to ensure that these are part of the official company records and not just part of "departmental history." Managers and supervisors sometimes move on to new jobs or change positions within the company, so the person who commended you for your valuable contribution to a particular project may not be there any longer when you volunteer for the next opportunity. Performance reviews are a good opportunity to prepare your own self-evaluation that addresses how you contributed to advancing the company's mission and objectives and summarizes your contributions to larger projects, and provides your manager with a document that lists these, especially if you know that the person isn't very good at taking notes themselves. I would also wager that even if your boss does a good job remembering your achievements, there are likely many instances where your particular contributions to an overarching project are overlooked.

One day I was having lunch with a friend who worked at a big law firm, and she mentioned that they needed to hire an associate. I thought of someone who I knew was looking for stretch opportunities and recommended this person to my friend. At first, she was dubious. "Isn't he very young and inexperienced?" she asked. I was able to send her a list of his contributions that afternoon, and she was impressed enough to interview him and offer him the role. That would not have happened so easily if I had no record of his work.

LEARN HOW TO EFFECTIVELY TALK ABOUT YOUR CONTRIBUTION

Insight, analysis, enthusiasm, and appropriate questions about what's next create an impression of engagement and competence. If you are tracking your accomplishments and thinking about how they fit into the bigger picture, you'll be able to talk naturally and effectively about them with your managers and senior executives without bragging.

> Insight, analysis, enthusiasm, and appropriate questions about what's next create an impression of engagement and competence.

For many of us, it's challenging and calls us to overturn long-established habits, but it's an important skill to learn, especially for women. Growing up in Philadelphia, I was taught that girls like me should always be humble, neat, clean, diligent, polite, and avoid boasting at all costs. At home, my parents celebrated my achievements and fostered the belief that I could do anything I wanted, but outside our home it seemed as though the idea was for girls to be almost invisible. My mom knew how difficult it was to work hard and not gain recognition, and she taught my sister and me to share and applaud our own accomplishments, even if they weren't publicly celebrated anywhere else. I'm so grateful that she taught me to track my accomplishments for my own benefit, but it took many years before I was comfortable

99

talking about them openly, and I certainly did not fully appreciate why sharing my achievements publicly mattered. Learning how to do this not only opened up new opportunities for challenge and visibility, but it also built my confidence and ability to engage with others at networking events and functions. In fact, the benefits are very real. Talking about my achievements and credentials at networking events opened the door to two very different but attractive opportunities: a position as deputy director at the Museum of African American History in Detroit and a position as deputy general counsel at ACC in Washington, DC.

After I had worked at Sunoco for several years, I was considering the next stage in my career, and one of my ideas was to move to a nonprofit organization. I was already working on a degree in art history and had also completed postgraduate courses in nonprofit fundraising and management. I learned about the museum opportunity at a cocktail party and the position at ACC during a reception at ACC's annual conference. I had attended both events simply because I was hoping to hear about possible opportunities, and when I did, the fact that I practiced the habit of Take Credit enabled me to be confident enough to talk about both my qualifications and how they made me the perfect candidate for these opportunities.

WHEN SHOULD YOU TAKE CREDIT PUBLICLY?

Well-managed teams usually have regular planning and evaluation meetings during projects as well as a thorough postmortem when the project is complete. Often these meetings are just seen as milestone trackers to confirm that the project is meeting deadlines, but they're also Take Credit opportunities, especially when you are working on a team project. Whether you're the team leader or a contributing member, learning how to accept commendation without immediately deflecting it is a critical skill.

In addition to these meetings, there are also public opportunities to Take Credit, and this is where the opportunity to shine is most often dissipated.

I've attended hundreds of awards dinners, celebratory gatherings, and recognition events over the years and have determined that there are three main patterns of response.

1. "My team did an amazing job, and I couldn't have done it without them." This suggests that the leader was merely a figurehead because they instantly deflected all the praise away from themselves.

2. "Thank you. It was hard work and took some serious problem solving and innovation, but I am so proud to be recognized!" (And the speech continues with all the accomplishments and obstacles.) The impression is that this person carried out the whole project almost alone.

3. "Thank you. It was an enormous task; we overcame these challenges and obstacles, and it was a privilege to lead such a diligent and responsive team." This approach accepts the responsibilities of leadership and takes credit for the overall execution while also acknowledging the contributions of the team, often by name.

As you can see, it's not a matter of grabbing all the attention and credit to yourself and holding it there; it is a question of timing and judgment.

When I was at MCCA, I initiated a research project that explored the many reasons why women were underrepresented, especially in senior positions, in the legal profession. Many of the conclusions zeroed in on this issue of taking credit and willingness to raise a hand and volunteer for stretch assignments. The consequences are sometimes reflected in promotion and pay differentials between men and women because of disparities in performance evaluations and perceived contributions.

Adam Grant and Sheryl Sandberg cite a "sad reality in workplaces around the world: Women help more but benefit less from it."[11] In an article reflecting on this fact, Tracy Moore outlines the effect of gender stereotypes on everything from the demands made on professionals to the impact of their response on promotions, opportunities, and raises.[12] Her long-term solution is to raise boys to care more about pitching in and helping with the routine work. She also highlights the need for women (and, I would add, racial/ethnic minorities) to recognize this cultural reality, learn to strategically Take Credit for their contributions, and **not** permit them to remain invisible. Michelle Redfern also elaborates on how gender stereotypes affect career opportunities. She tells the story of a pivotal confrontation with her boss over his assumption that as the lone female executive in the meeting, it was her place to take the minutes. As a result of her challenge, her boss recognized his mistake, apologized, and learned from the experience.[13] Michelle's point is **not** to tell women to always

---

11   Adam Grant and Sheryl Sandberg, "Madam C.E.O., Get Me a Coffee," *New York Times*, February 6, 2015, https://www.nytimes.com/2015/02/08/opinion/sunday/sheryl-sandberg-and-adam-grant-on-women-doing-office-housework.

12   Tracy Moore, "Women at Work: We're Doing All the 'Office Housework, Too," *Jezebel*, February 10, 2015, https://jezebel.com/women-at-work-were-doing-all-the-office-housework-too-1684271715.

13   Michelle Redfern, "How I Said No (Disgracefully) and Why It Worked," blog post, MichelleRedfern.com, November 22, 2018, https://michelleredfern.com/how-i-said-no-disgracefully-and-why-it-worked/.

avoid "routine housekeeping" tasks like taking minutes, organizing meetings, ordering food, or mentoring staff and only pursue the "glamour" (i.e., strategic) jobs more often snapped up by men. Instead, she encourages both men and women to recognize how automatic this type of gender bias can be and to call it out. She also suggests that leaders should create a roster for both types of assignments to provide all members of staff with equivalent assignments of both types. I would take this even further: as Tracy Moore says, "There's no 'Shit I Do Quietly That Proves I'm Respected and Capable but Can't Really Back Up' section" on your résumé, but there's no reason why this information shouldn't be provided to your manager in a written self-assessment and incorporated as part of your performance review."[14]

MAKING THE MOST OF PERFORMANCE REVIEWS

I've noticed that many employees don't prepare as thoroughly as they could for performance reviews, and this can be extremely detrimental to your career. This is the ideal opportunity to make sure that your accomplishments are part of the organizational records, so prepare thoroughly and make it easy for your supervisor to submit documentation that gives appropriate credit as well as provides feedback so that you can address any deficiencies.

As well as documenting your contribution to important projects, this is the time to let your manager know what you are hoping to achieve in the upcoming period and what new challenges you are seeking. This will provide your manager with an opportunity to take note of your goals and point out any areas in which you need to

---

14   For more resources on taking credit, see http://www.TakeSixHabits.com/.

develop, particularly the qualifications or specific experience that you need to obtain. Hopefully, you are working at a company with a structured review process that draws out these important areas, but in any case, you should take responsibility for providing written documentation of your contribution for the organizational files and helping your supervisor to track your progress, goals, and aspirations. You should also be prepared to ask for advice, support, and suggestions for next steps, additional skills, or qualifications, as well as challenge assignments during your review and make note of these suggestions.

WHAT IF I MAKE A MISTAKE?

The notion of taking credit applies to taking responsibility for failures as well as successes, and how you handle mistakes and failures reveals a lot about your character. In many ways, managers are just as interested in knowing how a candidate faces failure and recovers from mistakes as they are in hearing about their successes. This is a classic interview question, and your interviewers are listening closely to discover whether you are the kind of person who owns up to responsibility for your mistakes and any leadership failure, whether you are sufficiently self-aware to admit what you might have done differently in hindsight, or whether you are prone to excuses and attempt to shift the blame onto others. Most of the time they are looking for people who are prepared to own their mistakes, exercise good judgment, and do whatever is possible to rectify the mistake.

When I took over as CEO and president of ACC, we were predominantly a US-centric organization with a small global presence and big goals to broaden our influence and create a truly global organization.

We decided that rather than sending holiday greetings, which would not resonate with everyone, we would send a greeting to reflect on the close of another year, because everyone likes to reflect as the new year approaches, so that would be more inclusive. We put a lot of thought into that year-end letter, which talked about being responsible stewards of the resources entrusted to us, working to continue to add value for our members, how much we looked forward to even more global events and interactions in the coming year, and highlighting some of the upcoming new programs and services. We also took care to schedule distribution for a good time in all time zones. A few weeks later, I received a note from a member from Australia to the effect that he wasn't bundling up at all in the cold or sipping hot chocolate watching a snowfall; in fact, he was enjoying surfing and sunbathing at the beach with his family, and perhaps we should be a little more mindful of the international community. Despite all of our care, we made a critical error on the graphics and illustrations that accompanied the letter. In Washington, DC, we experienced freezing temperatures and icy conditions in December, and our mistake was failing to think beyond our own situation. The member wasn't offended, but he was right to point out our mistake. This is also a great example of the importance of having a variety of people—diverse perspectives—at the table who are willing to speak up.

We didn't try to hide our mistake; we acknowledged it and apologized. But most importantly, we made sure that in the future, we had a more representative group looking over similar communications and thinking about it from the perspectives of people who aren't in our location and who aren't like us.

"YOU'VE GOT TO BE IN IT TO WIN IT!"

One of the outcomes from the MCCA research on women was the realization that women often read and act on job descriptions quite differently from men, and this has a direct bearing on whether they apply or not.

One day I overheard the following tirade: "Did you hear that Al got that senior position at XYZ Corporation? He doesn't have half of the qualifications they asked for, and he doesn't have nearly my level of experience. I just can't believe it!"

I have heard so many comments and stories like this over the years, and they are directly tied to this habit of taking credit as well as understanding the nature of a job description. Most job descriptions include three or four core criteria that are nonnegotiable plus some nice-to-have optional items. The only certainty is that if you don't apply, then you won't be considered for the role. Mandy had seen the same position listed, read the criteria, and assessed herself as only having six of the ten, so she decided not to risk applying. Al saw the same criteria, thought that he met four of them, was smart enough to learn the rest on the job, and decided to give it a shot, so he applied, and ultimately, he landed the position.

It seems that underrepresented minorities (especially women and people of color) are much less likely to apply if they don't think they are close to meeting all the criteria; they tend to be more risk averse. Majority men are more likely to go ahead and apply anyway. Instead of bemoaning a culture that makes it difficult for outsiders to move up the ladder, let us start taking the actions that will lead to change by giving ourselves credit for what we have done and being willing to put ourselves forward. After all, the worst that can happen is that you won't get the new role. But the act of putting yourself in the running does force higher-ups to take note of your ability, experience, and achievements, and the value of that should never be underestimated ... and who knows? You might just be the one who lands the opportunity, either this time or in the future.

OVERCOMING OBSTACLES SO YOU CAN TAKE CREDIT MORE EFFECTIVELY

As you read through this book, I hope that you'll have moments when you pat yourself on the back and say, "I'm already doing that, and maybe I can get even better as I follow this book's advice," as well as other moments when you say to yourself, "I don't do this well at all, and I have a lot to learn." The one thing I never want you to say is, "I'm terrible at this; no wonder I can't get ahead."

LABELS AND BELIEFS

I've noticed that this habit of taking credit is one where many people say, "I can't change. It's just not my personality to brag and talk about my achievements."

Remember Sheila? That was the type of excuse she clung to in order to explain why the right acknowledgments never flowed her way.

It led to jealousy, bitterness, distrust, and her eventual departure. To the best of my knowledge, she never asked for help in this area because she said to herself, "That's just the way I am, quiet and modest. I don't go around bragging like Jack."

Sheila labeled people who shared word of their accomplishments or claimed credit for good results as braggers or self-promoters, and she didn't want to claim that label for herself. If that's how you think about it, you will have trouble as well, but if you thought about it as taking ownership of your work, would that change your attitude? If you thought of it as sharing information that others need to know about how the results were achieved, would that help to change your approach? The labels we assign have a very powerful influence on our actions, and they also shape our beliefs.

BUT THAT WAS MY IDEA!

Have you ever shared an idea with a colleague and then discovered that they've offered it as their own and are taking the public credit for it? Sometimes it's a perfectly innocent mistake born from the quirks of memory that cognitive neurologist Donna Bridge[15] described, and your colleagues may genuinely think that the idea was theirs. If it happens once, it may be an accident, but if it happens twice, then you should consider preparing an outline and sharing it with meeting attendees or your manager to preempt your colleague and stop them from promoting themselves at your expense.

SPEAK UP AND STAY CENTRAL

If you don't speak up and share your ideas readily in meetings or take part in conversations, then it's hard for others to take your contributions seriously or believe that you are engaged. You cannot claim credit for an idea or outstanding contribution if you are not prepared to make one. Prior to every meeting, take time to read any materials

---

15   For Donna Bridge's interesting work on memory, visit her website at http://www. DonnaJoBridge.com.

that have been circulated in advance, go over the agenda and objectives, and jot down any points you want to make or questions you wish to pose. In essence, being able to Take Credit is dependent upon the ability to show up prepared to contribute. How frequently are you showing up without having taken the time to bring your best to the discussion? How many meetings do you call without circulating an agenda first to clarify the objectives? How frequently do you just sit there listening without attempting to meaningfully contribute to the discussion? In addition to helping to frame the discussion and assist the meeting to run in a more timely and efficient manner, an agenda serves another goal—it is a framework you can use to reflect in advance and can give you and the other participants the opportunity to prepare appropriate and well-thought-out contributions.

> You cannot claim credit for an idea or outstanding contribution if you are not prepared to make one.

THE IMPORTANCE OF TAKING CREDIT

One of the things that stands out to me about taking credit for your accomplishments and achievements is its role in building your own confidence in your abilities and the confidence of those around you. This is not merely about patting yourself on the back so that you feel good about your work ethic and the effort you put in; it's also about seeing yourself as competent, talented, and capable so that you are willing to step up and face new challenges.

In the next chapter, we'll look at the habit of Take a Hand, which focuses on achieving your full potential by extending your hand to seek assistance or guidance as well as reach out your hand to assist someone else to move forward.

Because Jack has perfected the art of taking credit and recognizes his own contributions, he believes that he deserves a hand and feels confident asking for advice, and he is ready to explain why he deserves people's time and attention. In addition, his widely shared accomplishments also mean that other people (both internal and external to the organization) look to Jack for assistance and advice, which he recognizes as a positive reflection on how he is regarded. Sheila, however, struggled to claim credit for her genuine accomplishments and had an even harder time explaining to others why she deserved their influence or assistance. Because her contributions weren't recognized, people did not think to come to her for advice and assistance, either, so it became a vicious cycle of impotent frustration.

In the same way, your ability to celebrate your contributions and Take Credit for them will affect your ability to Take a Hand.

IN CHAPTER 4 YOU LEARNED:

- Adopting the essential habit Take Credit effectively opens the door for opportunities.
- It's your responsibility to learn to Take Credit rather than wait for other people to take notice of how wonderful you are.
- Recognition is a gift that you need to learn to accept, especially if it doesn't come naturally, and there is a way to do so with humility and grace.
- Women generally have a much harder time taking credit for their accomplishments than men do, so I especially

encourage all of the women reading this book to avoid that trap.

- It can be helpful to think of taking credit as simply taking ownership of your work and sharing positive results, and this mindset will prevent you from feeling like you are bragging.

TAKE SIX

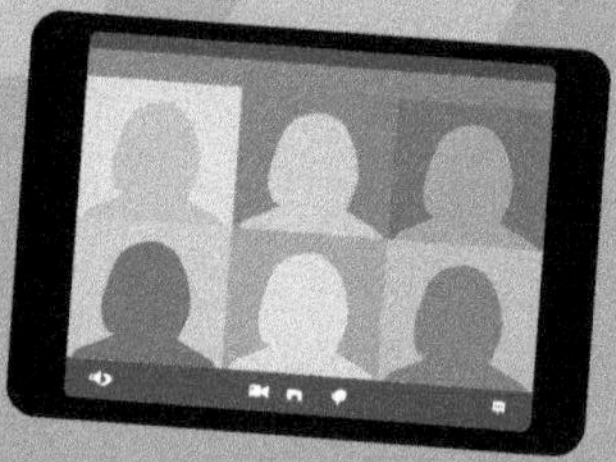

CHAPTER FIVE

TAKE A HAND

You are where you are today because you stand on somebody's shoulders. And wherever you are heading, you cannot get there by yourself. If you stand on the shoulders of others, you have a reciprocal responsibility to live your life so that others may stand on your shoulders. It's the quid pro quo of life. We exist temporarily through what we take, but we live forever through what we give.

—VERNON JORDAN

"Can we catch up for a quick lunch, Veta? I have something important to say that can't wait."

I didn't fully realize it at the time, but that brief invitation from a mentor represented an incredibly selfless act that inspires me to this day. On a rainy Friday in April, a member of President Barack Obama's circle of advisors sat down with me over lunch at Chef Geoff's restaurant. It had only recently been announced that I was selected as the incoming CEO of ACC, and after the expected congratulations on my new role and some brief chitchat, he jumped straight into the real reason for our meeting. He described a situation he once faced, when he came into a new organization as an outsider and discovered much later that there had been a disappointed internal candidate for the role to which he had been newly appointed. He then advised me to be sensitive to the possibility that I was walking into a similar situation, in which an unsuccessful candidate for my role might seek to undermine my selection, my qualifications, and my reputation. "If you want to succeed in your new role," he said, "you have to make sure that this type of situation is addressed sooner rather than later because otherwise you will have to deal with it during the early days of your tenure, and that will distract you from your mission."

Shortly afterward, he excused himself to go to a meeting at the White House. It was raining. I watched him walk out of the restaurant and pop his umbrella. A black sedan pulled up at the curb, my mentor climbed in, and the car took off in the direction of Pennsylvania Avenue.

I knew my mentor was juggling multiple weighty crises, most involving difficult and delicate issues of national and global security. The fact that he had taken time out of his busy schedule and onerous responsibilities to generously make me aware of a situation that could have sandbagged my opportunity and countered my ability to succeed in the role is something I remember and cherish to this day. His professional advice on how to handle this situation in the best interests of the organization and my own vision was insightful, constructive, and wise. Without going into the specific details, thanks to his generous advice, appropriate action was taken to address the challenge, any bad-mouthing ceased, and I have gone on to successfully lead ACC and expand its global reach.

I've thought about that incident many times since then, because it is a striking example of the value of supportive relationships with people who will watch your back and offer a helping hand, even when you haven't requested one and don't realize that help is needed. This man was never a person to whom I reported formally or even a coworker, yet he was part of my informal network of advisors and willing to sacrifice his time and energy to help me succeed in my new position. I've thought about this unforgettable example often when I've been presented with opportunities to advise or support others and wondered whether they'd appreciate the help, or whether I had the time to act on my hunch that someone needed to Take a Hand. The kindness I received always inspires me to go the extra mile.

TAKING A HAND IS A TWO-WAY STREET

Taking a hand. Mentoring. Advising. Buddy system ...

They're all different ways of expressing the need to build a support team and a network of advisors and role models who will invest in helping you become more effective and stay on track. I've lost count of the number of people who reached out a helping hand to me over the years, but their faces and the impact of what they offered are now ingrained in my mind. Their advice to me now influences the advice that I offer to others, whether it is given formally or informally. Like the

> You must develop the habit of reaching out to others to ask for their assistance as well as extending your hand to help someone else. Doing both is essential to your ability to optimize your full potential.

other essential habits that I share in this book, some ways of extending and taking a hand have more effect than others, and some situations demand more time-intensive efforts to reach out. But the bottom line is that you must develop the habit of reaching out to others to ask for their assistance as well as extending your hand to help someone else. Doing both is essential to your ability to optimize your full potential.

My mentor in the opening story could simply have spoken about the situation on the phone or written me a note to warn me about a potential situation I could be walking into, emphasize my need to act decisively, and given me some advice on how to do so appropriately. In the context of the global issues he was dealing with, any leadership challenges I was walking into were relatively insignificant, but he made three important decisions:

1. To reach out and give a hand for my personal benefit and for the good of the organization that I was preparing to lead

2. To use the most effective way possible to communicate his advice so that I would pay attention and not underestimate the consequences of inaction

3. To generously share his own experiences and admit the hard lessons he had learned about dealing with "haters" so that I could draw lessons from his experience in order to plot my pathway

In this chapter we'll look at how to build a network of advisors to whom you can turn when you need a hand, how to identify opportunities where you can be the person reaching back and helping others climb up, and why this is such an important habit to develop.

There's a lot of talk these days about "self-made success," which I find both comical and breathtakingly arrogant. From my perspective, one of the side benefits of the habit Take a Hand is its role as the important antidote to the temptation to believe that you've achieved success entirely on your own without help from others. At the very least, there were people in your life (parents, teachers, mentors, employers, and so on) who believed in your abilities, gave you opportunities to learn and grow, and offered you the gift of time, attention, and support (financial or otherwise). Any business owner or employer realizes that without clients, skills, relationships, and capital, they would never have reached their current level.

Another benefit of Take a Hand is that helping another person actually triggers positive physical benefits: it is good for both your physical and mental health. When you help other people achieve their goals, your body releases a shot of dopamine (the "feel-good" chemical) to your brain, which not only improves your self-esteem and makes it more likely that you will repeat the same action again, but also increases your happiness and motivation to succeed.[16]

The most popular course in the history of Yale University is Psychology 157: Psychology and the Good Life, taught by Professor Laurie Santos. While I have not been fortunate enough to attend this course, it is the subject of many articles and analysis. Professor Santos expresses an important truth that is central to most religious and moral teaching: "We assume that self-care looks like a nice bubble bath—or even hedonistic pursuits, selfish pursuits, but the data suggests that the right way to treat ourselves would be to do nice things for other people. We actually get more out of being more open and more social and more other-oriented than spending money

---

16   Dariush Dfarhud, Maryam Malmir, and Mohammad Khanahmadi, "Happiness and Health: The Biological Factors—Systematic Review Article," *Iranian Journal of Public Health* 43, no. 11 (2014): 1468–77; Friederike Fabritius and Hans W. Hagemann, *The Leading Brain: Powerful, Science-Based Strategies for Achieving Peak Performance* (Penguin Books, 2018), Chapter 1.

on ourselves. It's a bigger increase to your happiness."[17] There it is. Helping others is critical to our own happiness.

The purpose of this book is to help you reach your goals faster, enjoy life more along the way, and become the greatest possible version of yourself. If this is to be your destiny, you will find it absolutely necessary to seek models and advisors along your path who will reach out a hand to help you, and you will also discover opportunities to reach out to help others as well. Who knows? You may also have the chance to give back to the very people who helped you when you needed a hand.

When I worked at MCCA, its mission was to increase diversity within the legal profession. One of the initiatives I started was a scholarship program to support high-performing, high-potential students from diverse backgrounds who needed financial assistance to attend law school and achieve their dream of becoming an attorney. Although this initiative was launched under my watch, a lot of very generous corporations like Microsoft, DuPont, Walmart, and more provided the funding that actually made it happen.

Haris was one of the inaugural scholarship recipients and the type of young man who made an immediate positive impression. He graduated from law school with distinction and then went to work in a big, prestigious law firm where he quickly fine-tuned his legal skills, mastered complex substantive areas, and recognized the value he brought to the table. Over the years, we would talk periodically as Haris took stock regularly with the goal of opening greater professional opportunities for himself. I was proud to serve as a reference for Haris as he mulled over a couple of terrific in-house counsel opportunities

---

17   Sophie Downes, "How to Keep Your Employees Healthy While They're Working from Home," *Inc.*, October 6, 2020, https://www.inc.com/sophie-downes/remote-work-home-ergonomics-stress-back-pain-health.html.

at top-rated high-tech companies. Ultimately, he chose to accept a position in the Google (now Alphabet) law department, where he is continuing to develop his skills and expertise and was recently promoted to a senior position.

Haris played it smart. He did not squander the relationships he made through his experience as an MCCA scholar and his subsequent position as in-house counsel. Over the intervening years, he stayed in touch with people he met, supported their events and programs, and generously shared his advice and influence with others. When I moved to ACC and the Education Team wanted to invite Laszlo Bock, then SVP of People Operations at Google, to present a keynote address at our annual conference, we looked for someone to help ensure the request to speak reached Laszlo by personally dropping off a letter of invitation to his office, to increase the possibility that the letter might actually be read and seriously considered. It wasn't an easy task to get on the radar of such a high-profile leader. Several senior executives with whom ACC had a relationship and who were likely closer to Laszlo Bock were reluctant to act on this matter, but as soon as we asked Haris to take the letter of invitation to Laszlo's office, he said yes. He personally hand delivered the letter of invitation, and soon after the letter reached him, Laszlo Bock accepted.

Many of those who attended the event still talk about the outstanding keynote address Bock delivered, and the fact that he stayed after his speech to sign copies of his best-selling book *Work Rules!* made it especially

The lesson to be learned is that the person you help today may one day be in a position to help you in return.

memorable. None of that would have been possible without Haris agreeing to help. The lesson to be learned is that the person you help today may one day be in a position to help you in return. Although that should never be the reason you help someone, it's uncanny how karma works!

TAKING A HAND: A CLOSER LOOK

Take a Hand involves both extending a hand to help others and reaching out to others for help: two sides of the same coin. Whenever you invest your time and energy in another person, you receive a measurable "happiness boost," but you often also end up with greater clarity as a result of your efforts to communicate. It's like they say about the best way to master any skill or topic:

- Hear it explained.

- Watch someone do it.

- Practice it.

- Teach it.

In this chapter I'm going to focus on what it looks like when you **Take** a Hand, but I'd like you to remember that the obverse is also relevant and that it's never too early to reach back and extend a hand to others, because doing that helps you see how far you've already come.

From the examples you've already read in this chapter, Take a Hand could look like

- acting on advice that you did not request,

- accepting scholarships and opportunities for education and advancement,

- taking advantage of internships and networking opportunities to develop connections,

- going out of your way to make impactful introductions,

- listening to others' hard-won experiences and strategies so you can move ahead faster and avoid their mistakes, or

- reaching out and asking for advice and opportunities.

Early in my career, it felt as though I was always reaching out to others and asking for help because I knew I had such an enormous mountain to climb—one that I could never climb without substantial assistance. I had so much to learn and do, and I was acutely aware of how much I needed help to accomplish my dreams and goals. In those days, part of my taking stock process included lists of people to meet and specific questions I wanted them to answer, as well as ever-growing lists of the skills and educational or professional qualifications that would be helpful. In addition to all the questions that any aspiring lawyer needs to know, I had specific questions for professionals who were African American and/or women about how to navigate effectively in the face of unique situations and challenges that accompany being a member of these underrepresented sectors of my profession.

It is extremely important to keep your eyes open for informal mentors and role models.

Formal guidance and mentoring programs aren't always as effective as they are intended to be, as I discovered when I consulted the guidance counselor at the University of Maryland about fast-tracking my undergraduate degree, but they are worth investigating. However, it is extremely important to keep your eyes open for informal mentors and role models. In my first year of college, my best friend, Cheryl Thompson, was a sophomore, and she helped me design my course and workload so that I could finish my undergraduate education in just three years.

As I was writing this chapter and reflecting on those early days when I felt as though I was always stretching my hand out to those ahead of me and asking for help, two important principles jumped out at me:

1. When you are actively seeking and accepting help, you are very conscious of the need to pay it forward.

2. When you share your discoveries and experience with others, it sharpens and clarifies your own thinking. Thus, the act of helping another sharpens your powers of assessment and problem solving, allowing you to build "muscle memory."

Because of the challenges I experienced when I was trying to design my accelerated degree, when incoming freshmen asked me what it involved, I was happy to help them with course selection and other elements of their studies. I also made a point of sharing the lessons I had learned from Cheryl about coping with workloads and making time for the social activities and good times that make college days so memorable. The process of sitting down with someone, discovering their reasons for acceleration, explaining the ins and outs of the process, and helping them consider all the implications of their choices helped me realize how much I had learned and reinforced my own decision to accelerate my degree.

As I progressed through law school, I was very deliberate about the events that I attended and relationships I cultivated (especially once I had developed my conversation and networking skills, as discussed in chapter 2). My goal was to build a broad network of relationships for the long haul and not merely to focus on someone's apparent short-term "usefulness" because it's a mistake to view any relationship as merely transactional. Recently, someone asked me how to determine whom to stay in touch with and how to do so. We'll talk about the "how" later on in this chapter, but I want to emphasize the importance of being strategic in your networking relationships. Strategic networking involves doing research and discovering who are key professionals or experts in your field, and then seeking opportunities to meet and stay in touch with those people. It also includes pursuing relationships with less-well-known people with whom you share interests and simply enjoy being around. The reality is that you never know where someone's career will take them and how they may have a chance to help you later on, so it makes sense to be polite and interested in everyone you meet, while investing extra effort in relationships that you enjoy.

One of my role models for being a giving, supportive mentor is Tom Sager, the now-retired former general counsel of DuPont Company, who, in spite of his demanding responsibilities, has always been the kind of man who gives whenever it is in his power to do so. Tom was on the MCCA board of directors for many years and was a strong and early proponent of diversity in the legal profession as well as one of the most influential general counsels and top innovators for how to reframe the relationship between in-house counsel and the law firms they retain. Time, advice, practical assistance—Tom was alert to opportunities to challenge and raise people's aspirations and to lend them a hand or give them a boost to support their goals. At networking events and conferences, Tom could often be found talking to younger lawyers, many of whom would return to work with renewed focus and enthusiasm as a result of their conversation with him and the practical suggestions he offered to help them Take Stock of their aspirations.

From my perspective, Tom was the ultimate example of how "too busy" and "too important" can simply be code words for "can't be bothered." When you asked to talk to Tom, you might have to wait a few days or weeks for an appointment, but you always knew that he would be 100 percent focused on you during that time, and that he would do his best to provide the advice or assistance you needed. He taught me the importance of making time for others and giving generously.

I learned an equally important lesson from Ann Mulé during my early years at Sunoco. Ann was the mentor assigned to us during the internship program at Sunoco, and when I started working there, she took me under her wing. If you had asked me who I wanted to be in those days, I would have said, "I want to be like Ann." She continued to give me critical guidance and mentoring throughout my time there. In the early days, I was desperate to fit in and make a good impression, so I resolved to study up on the latest sports news and try to get a grasp of the games. Baseball, football, basketball, and so forth really had no burning interest for me, but I thought they would make good topics of conversation. After hearing me laboriously try to hold my end up in a conversation about basketball at a social event, Ann took me aside and gave me some advice that has stuck with me: "Veta, don't pretend to be interested in sports when you aren't really. Just be yourself and admit that you don't follow these things. If you pretend that you're interested in them, people will quickly discover that you really don't know what you're talking about, and that will undermine their trust in you."

Ann went on to tell me a story about her first few months at Sunoco as a young lawyer. She, like me, was anxious to fit in, earn people's respect, and be taken seriously, so when she went on business trips with colleagues, she would buy a business magazine to read for appearances' sake, but she would have the current issue of *People* magazine that she was actually reading hidden inside it. Eventually, she realized that some of her colleagues also read *People* magazine, so she dropped the pretense and found that she had more natural conversations around topics that both parties were interested in. She helped me to see that you can be genuinely interested in how other people think and what interests them about various topics they care about (like sports, music, movies) without having to pretend that you know or follow the topic for its own sake.

Following Ann's example and the lessons I had learned at college, when interns or new hires arrived at Sunoco, I would actively reach out to help them find their feet and succeed in this new environment. It wasn't a question of advising them on career moves, but of making them aware of undercurrents of office politics, unwritten rules of the department, how to approach certain situations, or the complexities of working with internal clients. I learned a lot from people's responses to these efforts to help them adjust, just as I later learned a lot from people's responses to performance reviews.

Throughout my career, I've found that performance reviews can be extremely valuable ... or they can be a waste of time. When someone offers meaningful, constructive feedback that you can use to further your progress, that's a gift, especially if you are already doing well, because you can use it to do even better and contribute more significantly. When you're eager to succeed and face new challenges with confidence, hearing, "Good job!" will provide short-term satisfaction and make you feel good. But if that's the only feedback you receive, it may not be particularly helpful over the longer term. You want to seek additional feedback to understand the ways that you can improve. It's important to be able to assess your strengths as well as areas where you may need additional focus.

Recently, a young man named Jonathan reached out to me and asked if he could invest the next few months volunteering at ACC. He had just graduated from law school, his bar exam date had been postponed due to the COVID-19 disruptions, and his start date at a prestigious law firm had been moved back several months. Rather than just leisurely passing the time, Jonathan saw this delay as an opportunity to learn, develop new skills, and expand his network of contacts so that he could build relationships that might turn into genuine recommendations or help advance his future professional opportunities. His initiative and desire to invest in himself was impressive.

Jonathan's initiative in creating an opportunity to learn shows that he's already thinking strategically, taking stock of his situation, and ready to ask for help so that he can fill the gaps. His plans for the near future were disrupted, and there was a great deal of uncertainty about what might happen next. Along with the rest of his cohort, there was a strong probability that he would have to navigate a difficult economy, and he smartly sought to control whatever he could, especially how to spend this unexpected time. Volunteering with ACC was one way he could build his résumé and network in the midst of these challenges. I had previously met Jonathan when I agreed to speak at a program he helped to organize at his law school, and among all the students to whom I gave my business card, Jonathan was the only one who made the effort to follow up and keep in touch.

When he came to me with his proposal to volunteer, he explained the careful thinking behind his request: the value of the work experience he would receive, the opportunities to see inside corporate law departments, the potential to build relationships with people who might be potential clients one day. For him, these benefits outweighed the money he might have earned elsewhere through a short-term paid opportunity, and it definitely was more productive than whiling away the time at the beach. Those were all excellent reasons by themselves, but he had another reason: "Veta, one day in the future, I might ask you for a reference or recommendation to someone. Right now, you can tell them that you know me and that I have a good track record, but if you have actually worked with me, you will be able to talk specifically about my work quality and work ethic."

The circumstances were slightly different, but it reminded me of the letter I had sent many years ago to Don Walsh at Sunoco requesting an unpaid internship in order to open new doors for myself. I suspect that Don Walsh felt the same willingness to extend a helping hand as I felt with Jonathan. It was a chance for me to pay forward the kindness I had experienced many years ago. And, by the way, Jonathan did such a terrific job as our first "ACC Fellow" that our organization is looking to continue to extend opportunities like this to future fellows.

> **With a little creativity and courage to craft your own opportunities, you have the ability to open doors for yourself and cultivate important new relationships.**

The lesson to be learned is that with a little creativity and courage to craft your own opportunities, you have the ability to open doors for yourself and cultivate important new relationships. Volunteering was the path that Jonathan and I chose, but what path will you pursue?

EVERYONE NEEDS TO TAKE A HAND

The power of each of the essential habits that this book focuses on is that they are universally applied and perennial. As a habit, Take a Hand doesn't look the same as it used to for me, but it's still part of my foundation and beliefs for navigating professionally.

When you Take Stock, you discover many things you need to learn and do, and you'll find many situations in which you really need to Take a Hand. Often, I'd ask for help for something specific and discover that I needed to learn "yet another" new skill or meet "yet another" person or explore "yet another" avenue. Updating that list of things to enhance, upgrade, and develop in my life became second nature because every time I came back from a networking event, conference, or meeting, I would have new items or contacts to add.

These days my list may not be as long, but I'm still learning and going deeper. In fact, when I look around at the successful people in every field, I realize that they're the ones who are always on the lookout for ways to improve existing skills and learn new ones. Often, Take a Hand these days means that I am reaching sideways to acquire new skills with the help of a colleague or even "down the career ladder" to the people who support the organization to discover how we could be more effective. Take a Hand is not always about reaching up to someone who is further up the hierarchy, but that's often how it is narrowly and mistakenly interpreted.

At the start of your career, when you move into a new role, or when you are making a change, you need help to learn how to navigate your environment and to look ahead for next steps. For me as a young lawyer, this meant seeking guidance from the in-house senior legal team, getting to know and work with as many people as possible and tapping into their expertise and relationships, attending conferences, studying securities and finance law, and actively pursuing relationships so that I could eventually attain a seat on a for-profit board. I'm still in contact with many of the people I met and learned from during those earlier years, and I still value their advice. Some of them, like the mentor I talked about at the start of this chapter, pop back into my life unexpectedly to offer counsel I didn't even know I needed. At other times, I'm deliberately reaching out to people for advice, coaching, or support because I'm always taking stock and recognizing my need to grow.

As you move into different roles and become more senior, you may discover that you need to Take a Hand and get some coaching so that you can develop the skills you need to be even more effective. I'm the kind of person who often starts thinking aloud and exploring ideas. For many years, I was in supporting roles in which I could express a thought without anyone thinking that I had the seniority and authority for that to be a decision, but early in my tenure as a chief executive, we were discussing the organization's annual conference. We had reviewed the preceding conference and were making plans for the following year in light of our learnings, and I made what I intended as a discussion-starter comment about the possibility of holding it in a different city. To my surprise, my comment was interpreted as a decision that caused others to issue directives, and people had been tasked with researching facilities, accommodations, et cetera. When I learned about the venue decision, I realized the confusion caused by my communication style and decided I needed to find someone to help me improve, because effective communication is critical for leaders. So I hired an executive coach to help me. The solution my coach suggested to this was as simple as prefacing this kind of discussion with the clarifying prompt, "I am just thinking out loud here," sharing my thoughts, and then inviting others to contribute and also clearly communicating any decision as such. It sounds so simple, yet I needed to take the hand of an executive coach to determine what was needed and how I should change.

TAKING A HAND IS ABOUT ATTITUDE AS MUCH AS ANYTHING

What kind of person do you want to be?

What kind of world do you want to live in?

What part do you want to play in the making of that world?

No matter who we are or what position we hold, we all make choices about these things on a daily basis. These choices make a great deal of difference to the people around you, and I've noticed that people who don't readily ask for help often have a hard time helping others. BK Fulton and his wife, Jackie Stone, are good friends of mine. Jackie has been recognized multiple times for being an amazing mentor and has won awards for her many contributions to enrich the professional lives of others. Jackie sent me the link to the inspiring commencement address that BK delivered virtually to the graduates of the DaVinci Center in May 2020. In this address, BK shared a little-known story about world-renowned physicist Albert Einstein as a lesson in the importance of kindness and befriending those in need.[18]

Einstein chose to speak at HBCUs far more frequently than at other institutions because, in the mid- to late 1930s, when German Jews were trying to escape Hitler's Germany and needed jobs to apply for US residency, HBCUs offered many of them jobs to help rebuild their lives. Einstein so deeply respected that action and appreciated the values it demonstrated that he invested his time and energy toward the education of HBCU students who jumped at the chance to learn from one of the greatest minds of the twentieth century.

---

18 BK Fulton, VCU DaVinci Center Commencement, May 9, 2020. https://www.youtube.com/watch?v=giimCcWsFWU.

While I am certainly no Einstein, in the legal profession, a lot of people seek me out for advice and mentoring, which I am willing to provide as frequently as possible. These people might be colleagues, consultants, or students, and I see these as mutual opportunities to help each other grow and provide constructive advice and helpful suggestions. I'm also approached by young professionals who ask if I would be willing to engage in a more formal mentoring relationship. I am always happy to help others get clarity and discover their next steps, but I am also aware that my time and energy are finite, so I am looking for people who share my desire to create a world in which every person has the opportunity to fulfill their potential and who want to succeed so they can be part of that bigger goal.

Recently, a colleague I've known for many years in leadership roles found himself between jobs in a tough market. He contacted me to let me know he was looking for a new position, and I agreed to keep alert for opportunities to pass along word of them to him. But beyond asking for my help to support his job search, he also asked how he might be helpful to any projects or people that I might recommend. Since he had a lot of experience as corporate counsel and I had recently started advising a young woman at a law firm who was seeking to move in-house, I asked this colleague if he would be willing to speak with her. He was happy to do so, and the young woman ended up receiving advice from another experienced lawyer in addition to hearing my perspective. When you are known as a person who makes helpful introductions, it doesn't just feel good, but it also helps to positively extend your influence and impact.

In the legal profession in which I have worked for the past few decades, a woman named Laurie Robinson Haden has become legendary for the ability to Take a Hand. Laurie founded a now-global network called Corporate Counsel Women of Color (CCWC) to enable racial/ethnic minority women to connect with and support one another. The events are amazing and empowering because women who are often in the minority in their workplaces come together for a conference experience with rooms filled with peers who are like them. For the women and men who are not racial/ethnic minorities and attend CCWC programs, it's a paradigm shift from the typical legal-conference experience. Laurie's initiative to launch CCWC was born of her own experience, starting first as a group of women lawyers of color getting together for dinner, and the dinner group grew by word of mouth. Then Laurie took the risk to organize a first conference, and its success fueled the next, eventually becoming a powerhouse event. Laurie's story as a leader and strategist is a reminder of how one committed person can positively impact and build a community in which taking a hand and supporting one another becomes the norm.

HOW YOU CAN TAKE (AND GIVE) A HAND EFFECTIVELY

INTRODUCTIONS

The ability to make introductions is extremely powerful, so it's important to do it correctly and not to abuse your relationship. Always ask permission before you introduce someone

Don't earn your kindness chips with someone else's effort.

if you are planning to request their assistance for another, and don't mention it to the other person until you have permission to make the introduction so that you aren't assuming their willingness to help. Otherwise, you may end up embarrassing yourself and the influential person whose help you were seeking on behalf of your contact. Just follow the rule, "Don't earn your kindness chips with someone else's effort."

A few years ago, a friend in the literary arts community said that he would be happy to speak with students who have an interest in the arts anytime and to let me know whenever there was someone whom he might be able to help. I thought of this open offer when I was advising a student who was looking for some connections in the arts community to further his career. I reached out to confirm that my friend was still willing and able to do this. It took a while to hear back, which was unusual, and when he eventually replied, his response was, "No. Not right now." I learned that his wife was ill and that he was also recovering from an injury, so it was simply not a good time. I was so glad that I had reached out before I raised the student's expectations and put my friend in an uncomfortable position. I then focused on contacting others who were able to help the student at that time.

Most people are really careful about how they introduce people to other influential people, but not everyone is. At an event last year, I overheard the following introduction: "Hi, I want you to meet Lisa. She's had five years' experience in your field, and she's interested in working for XYZ Company. I told her about all the people you know at XYZ Company and that you would be able to introduce her to the right people."

I didn't hear all of the conversation after that, just enough to know that this was not a preplanned introduction. Maybe it was selfless and well intentioned—or maybe the person introducing Lisa wanted to impress her—I'm not certain. I do know that it felt presumptuous, and if Lisa had been introduced to me, I would have felt very uncomfortable being put on the spot at an event and "volun-told" to find a stranger a job without knowing anything about Lisa's experience or background. A similar incident happened to me when one of my mentees bragged to a friend about what a great mentor I was. His friend must have said that he would like to meet me, because out of the blue, I received an email from my mentee introducing me to his friend, telling me what his friend was hoping to achieve, and basically assigning me to "make it happen." In this case, I felt I had to speak up to let my mentee know he should always reach out to ask someone if it's OK to make an introduction like that. It is important to respect people's time and make it their decision whether they choose to help, not a directive.

It is important to respect people's time and make it their decision whether they choose to help, not a directive.

The situation with Lisa would have looked quite different if the introduction had been, "Hi, I want you to meet Lisa because I think you have a common interest in international energy corporations." The other person could then have made a choice about whether to help Lisa with an introduction after Lisa had cultivated the relationship a little.

A final comment on introductions: When I first started working at Sunoco, there would be occasions where I needed to reach out to someone I didn't yet know personally. My mentor, Ann, would often say, "I know X. Let me send them a note to let them know that you will be in touch."

I didn't understand the point of this at the time. It seemed unnecessary. After all, wouldn't my request receive just as much attention on its own merit? Now I realize that the answer is usually, "No, people don't pay as much attention without an introduction." Everyone is busy and inundated with requests, so an introduction from one trusted advisor to another signals to the recipient that it is important to make time for this particular individual.

FORMAL MENTORING AND BUDDY SYSTEMS

Many companies these days have formal mentoring or buddy systems, and programs like these can be very helpful if you see them as a resource and think through what help you might need (as the mentee) or be able to give (if you are the mentor). These sessions are not just random opportunities to chat aimlessly about sports or the weather, although they are opportunities to discover common interests; they are a chance for you to ask for information that is not directly related to particular tasks, to discover new resources and models, to build a list of skills to develop and learn about opportunities, and much, much more.

If you are on the mentoring end of the relationship, it is also a chance to guide your mentee. Help them learn all the things that you wish you'd known, as well as make it a personal Take Stock opportunity and see how far you have come. Many employers pair their new associates and interns with a buddy who is a year or so ahead of them. How you approach the opportunity to be a mentor and the effort you put into it speaks volumes about the kind of person you are, and the manager or supervisor you may have the potential to be. It can also represent one of those "wow" moments when you listen to their newbie questions and realize that you were asking those same questions just a year earlier, even though now your answers come naturally. I've noticed that the people who think that talking to a mentor is a waste of time because they're not actually getting work done are frequently the ones who have most difficulty reaching their goals. That time spent seeking guidance and building relationships is work, too, and it's important to the overall success of the employee and, ultimately, the organization for those conversations to take place.

CONFERENCES, CORPORATE EVENTS, AND OTHER OPPORTUNITIES TO CONNECT

At many corporate and nonprofit events, there are carefully selected sponsors and donors, and this offers another classic Take a Hand opportunity. Organizers are looking for sponsors who will benefit attendees, as well as ones to whom they can deliver value so that the sponsor and the organizer both feel that the event was worthwhile. You should seek to attend key industry conferences and use your time at these events wisely to network, expand your contacts, and build or reinforce relationships, recognizing that one or more of those relationships could result in a new mentor. Don't just focus on trying to talk to the speakers—everyone is trying to do that—so be smart about how you spend your time. Make sure that you visit the sponsor booths because these have been carefully curated and are a potential source of important information, resources, and introductions.

In addition, when you meet people at these events and they offer you their business card and invite you to stay in touch, these are genuine offers that are meant to be used if you think they could be helpful. That's what Jonathan did when he reached out to me and asked if he could help out at ACC. Hundreds of people have met me at any number of these events and ask for my business contact details. Very few of them actually reach out to me.

Charlie introduced himself to me at an MCCA event several years ago. He was one of the finalists for MCCA's scholarship award that year, and he wanted to let me know how much the scholarship would mean to him. I already knew his story from his application and was aware that this scholarship wasn't just going to make a difference to him, but it was also going to create opportunities for his siblings. I also already knew that he wasn't one of the scholarship recipients, and I wanted to help him. Before we parted ways after the event, I gave him my business card and said, "Charlie, I want to be your mentor. Whether you get the scholarship or not, call me if you need anything." I genuinely wanted to help him and was delighted when he followed up after learning that he hadn't received the scholarship. Over the next few months, we stayed in touch, and one day he called to ask for some advice: he was getting interviews, but no job offers or second interviews, and he couldn't figure out what was wrong. We met for coffee, and together we went over his résumé, interview technique, and answers to questions, and I really couldn't see what was wrong. He had great grades and a winning personality. Finally, I asked in desperation, "So what are you wearing to your interviews?"

Bingo! He was wearing an inexpensive black suit, and it was **not** working in his favor because he looked more like an undertaker than a lawyer.

We enlisted the help of Charlie's then-girlfriend, now wife, who had very good taste, to help him select the right professional attire. Dressed in a new gray suit, Charlie made a far better first impression, landed top-tier job offers, and made his way from there. Charlie has gone on to become quite an opportunity creator for others and hosts an annual technology conference at his HBCU alma mater, Howard Law School, where many of Charlie's professional contacts and colleagues from Microsoft volunteer their time to expose the students to current technology law issues and speak about their career path to a company like Microsoft. Charlie is a perfect example of how investing in a "giver" creates a ripple effect as he helps others who can then help others, and so on; that's how positive change happens.

PRACTICAL TIPS FOR CONFERENCES

Many people struggle to make connections at conferences. Either they end up talking to no one, or they talk to the people they already know. Here are some suggestions that will help you become more confident and comfortable:

1. Identify speakers in advance, and do some research on their backgrounds.

2. You may want to set up appointments in advance and arrange to meet people during a break. Don't be afraid to reach out to them; the worst they can do is ignore you or say no.

3. Try to sit toward the middle of the room, not on an aisle or on the edges of the auditorium. Say hello to those seated near you.

4. Talk to the sponsors, and visit their booths; they will often have great advice and may be able to introduce you to other great contacts.

5. The two most powerful questions you can ask someone whose success you aspire to emulate are, "What do you read to stay current in your field?" and "What networks do you participate in as essential for your work?" Then you read what they read and go where they go.

6. Prepare some open-ended questions to use in conversation, like, "Tell me, what brings you to this conference?" or "What program sessions or speakers have been standouts?"

It's interesting how conversations develop in different parts of the country and different cities. In Philadelphia, where I grew up, a typical conversation would start with, "What is your name?" Then you would be asked, "Where are you from?" because communities are close knit, and being a local native earns points. And finally, "What do you do?" becomes another way to assess relationships you may have in common. After that, the conversation would either wither or flourish, depending on your conversational ability and mutual interests. By contrast, in Washington, DC, conversations are more likely to start with, "What do you do?" to size up whether the person could be helpful. Depending on your answer to that question, you might then get asked, "Where do you live?" so they can assess your neighborhood and thus how well you must be doing financially to live there. And if you get asked, "What is your name?" then you know that you have passed their suitability test. Guess which model helps you develop better relationships and enjoy your networking more? I may live and work in the Washington, DC, region but I definitely avoid following the regional conversational pattern.

WHO AND WHAT ARE YOU LOOKING FOR?

Take a Hand grows from Take Stock. You don't need to know exactly what you want, as I did, in order to reach out and ask for a hand. In fact, in many ways it's easier to Take a Hand right at the start when your options are still very broad, because there are lots of people who can help you winnow your choices and direct how you focus by asking the right questions.

You don't need to know exactly what you want, as I did, in order to reach out and ask for a hand.

As you narrow down your interests and move deeper, you'll start to develop a list of specific subjects and fields, possibly even companies who operate in your fields of interest. At this point it's a good idea to start following the issues online and learning as much as possible about the current people, issues, trends, and politics.

In normal times, you'll be networking and attending events (remember that in-house events are opportunities too), and I suggest that you keep a list of people you talk to (business cards are very helpful for this) and topics of interest or things you learned. You can't remember everything, so the sooner you develop the habit of making notes in the contact records in your phone or on the backs of business cards you collect, the better.

Building relationships in your field is like building relationships in any large organization: you can't be best friends with everyone, but you can stay in touch strategically with a lot of people if you remain mindful, develop an organized approach to checking in, and commit to making an effort to do so. Put periodic reminders on your calendar or monthly schedule to prompt your follow-through. Harness your favorite form of technology to prompt you regularly.

Remember what I said at the start of this chapter? Don't just build useful or transactional relationships. If you only connect with people who are "important," then people will question your authenticity, and you will also lose many opportunities to connect with people who may later be in an ideal position to help you reach your goals. My personal practice is to try to make a few notes in the contact profile for everyone I have more than a passing conversation with. It helps to stay in touch and be able to personalize a follow-up note, even if it has been years since our first meeting. Of course, if you're working in the same field, it should be fairly easy to find common topics of conversation, as every professional appreciates being sent an article on a topic in their field or an invitation to an event that's relevant to their responsibilities.

TIPS FOR STAYING IN TOUCH

Here are a few ideas to get you started, but this is hardly an exhaustive list. With a little thought and ingenuity, I'm confident you can develop your own list of tips.

1. Make note of birthdays or work anniversaries (LinkedIn is very helpful at reminding you about these) and just reach out to send best wishes.

2. When you hear about someone's job change, contact them and congratulate them, and take a moment to add a personal touch to the note if only to reference the event at which you initially met or a restaurant recommendation in the new city to which they relocated.

3. If you discover you share a common passion or interest, then send them a relevant article or other information about the topic from time to time.

4. Ask for their opinion when you see something that you know they are interested in: you can send a quick note saying something like, "I saw the following article the other day and would be interested in your thoughts on it." This is an excellent opportunity to open discussion and make yourself relevant.

5. Make a point of sending the occasional message or email just to stay in touch and keep them up to date.

6. If you are making a request, make it specific, easy, and clear (if it looks as though I will need to spend hours researching something or write a lengthy essay, I probably won't respond).

7. NEVER let the first time you follow up after meeting someone

be to ask them for something that is extremely demanding or something that assumes a high degree of trust (like a job or an important introduction). That starts the relationship off on a needy note.

8. Develop chutzpah! Successful people are usually extremely generous with their time and advice if you ask for it. Inviting someone to have coffee and asking them questions is a powerful way to start a mentoring relationship and see where it goes from there.

IT'S NOT ROCKET SCIENCE!

The habit Take a Hand really boils down to a commitment to your own growth and to helping others grow too.

My parents lived this commitment out throughout my childhood, as I saw them contribute to the community through volunteering to help with organizations like Big Brothers and Girl Scouts, school trips, and beyond; giving a helping hand to their friends as often as possible (sometimes even without being asked); and making sure they were never too busy to stop and encourage those whom they knew and cared about. They also instilled in me the confidence to ask for help and made sure that I knew that being helped didn't excuse me from working hard and paying it forward.

Every day of my life, my mom demonstrated her belief in my ability to learn, grow, and succeed. Her encouragement and love were limitless, but they weren't casual. She expected me to grow. She taught me to aspire. She taught me to be grateful, even as I always reached for more. She also taught me that no failure is ever final … unless you quit. In the process, she showed me the importance of giving to others freely, but with discrimination, because there are people in this world who are pure takers (watch out for them!) and situations in which we need to Take a Stand and raise a voice to protest.

IN CHAPTER 5 YOU LEARNED:

- Take a Hand involves reaching out and asking for help as well as helping others to get what they need.
- Successful people are rarely too busy to help others, so it's up to you to reach out to them and ask for what you need.
- How to use conferences, seminars, and live events to find mentors and create connections.
- Practical ways to establish and maintain lasting relationships with an ever-growing network.

TAKE SIX

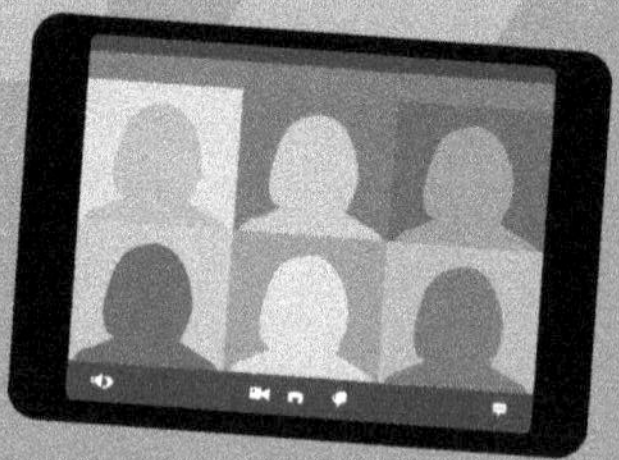

CHAPTER SIX

TAKE A STAND

We will not be satisfied until all of us—no matter what our age, our colour, our ethnic or religious origin, our sexual preference or our ability—are able to lead the lives we choose, free from discrimination and repression.

—ANNE SUMMERS, THE
WOMEN'S MANIFESTO[19]

"WTF!" I hollered as I flung the coveted invitation and accompanying flyer to the floor of my office.

"What is going on, Veta?" asked my assistant with alarm as she stood at the doorway looking at the papers on the ground. She had never seen me that angry and was concerned.

---

19   For the source of this quote, see Anne Summers's *The Women's Manifesto* presented at the Australian Education Union (Victorian Branch) International Women's Day, Melbourne, March 7, 2017, https://issimo.s3.amazonaws.com/static/thirdpartyassets/annesummers/TheWomensManifestopdffinal.pdf.

I stooped to pick up the papers and dropped them on my desk as she made her way over to take a look. There, staring up at us from the flyer, was Al Jolson in full blackface makeup posing in that minstrel costume, with the words "A Celebration of Al Jolson" emblazoned on a banner above the jarring image. Next to it was the memo, "Mr. and Mrs. Bob Campbell invite you to join them at the following event. Please RSVP to HR on or before ..."

"I can't believe this, but I was just invited to a **minstrel show**!" I choked, thoroughly outraged. "They tell me I am a high performer and to expect an invitation from the CEO, and then I receive this. Are they crazy?" My assistant shook her head in disbelief and closed my door as she exited.

After I had calmed down a little, I decided I would RSVP to the designated HR manager as requested. I called her extension. Her assistant answered. She was not available. So I opted to leave a message on voice mail: "Hi, this is Veta Richardson. I received the event invitation today and am RSVPing to let you know that I have decided to decline. As a Black person, I am not comfortable to attend this celebration of Al Jolson. In case you may not realize it, Black people consider blackface minstrel shows very offensive, as it's an ugly reminder of America's racist history. Thank you. Goodbye."

My response apparently caused quite a stir, and someone from HR quickly called me back and went into "syrupy-sweet mode" to smooth things over, apologize, and ask me to drop the invitation and flyer into an interoffice memo and return it to her. She went on to explain that no one had intended any disrespect, they hoped I would accept the apology, and they would like to send another invitation to a different event that they hoped I would consider attending.

Not long after, another invitation from the office of the CEO was delivered to my inbox. This time, I had been invited to a black-tie fundraiser, and my significant other and I would be seated at the same table as the CEO and his wife. I accepted.

That evening as we walked to find our table, Bob asked to speak with me privately for a moment. He personally apologized for the offensive invitation, taking full responsibility, explaining that when he heard what happened, he was not happy that Sunoco was supporting a local theater that would choose that event for its seasonal offerings, and steps had been taken to ensure that closer attention was paid to future sponsorship choices. I sighed with relief and thanked him as we joined his wife and my guest at the Sunoco table. We had a lovely evening and spent time exchanging stories and getting to know one another. I had a memorable time.

I was impressed by Bob's readiness as a leader to own the mistake, apologize, take corrective action, and move forward. The truth is, we both knew he had not personally picked out that event or prepared my invitation. Yet he did not hesitate to be accountable and say he was sorry; he also never mentioned the role anyone else may have played. It was a lesson in how leaders hold themselves accountable for everything—especially the mistakes—without trying to pass the buck or point a blaming finger at a subordinate. Now, as a leader myself, it's an approach I've adopted. Mistakes happen. Responses matter.

Many of my colleagues were shocked at my forthright action. In their minds, no thirty-year-old with a career ladder to climb should even contemplate calling out the CEO, but I didn't even consider not speaking up about that offensive invitation. In addition to learning a lesson about leadership myself, I feel I taught Sunoco's management a lesson that would help them to review future sponsorship requests so that they would be more carefully evaluated.

"DO YOU REALLY EXPECT *ME* TO TAKE A STAND AGAINST *THEM*?"

Yes, actually I do.

Remember how I talked about how my mentor challenged me to "be authentic" because that would reinforce people's belief that I could be trusted in chapter 3, "Take Risk"? When you Take a Stand rather than let others demean your values, beliefs, or heritage, you are being authentic ... and that builds trust. For many people, the habits of taking risk and taking a stand are very much interrelated because their courage and curiosity make these habits essential to how they view themselves and approach their lives. That's certainly true of my sister, Vicki, for whom the biggest risk is standing still and not taking on a significant new challenge or change every couple of years. That's her authentic way of being, just as it's also part of her DNA to speak up for herself and for others whose rights need a champion.

In this chapter, we'll talk about why taking a stand is important for your personal growth, how it can help your career, the potential cost of taking a stand, as well as the cost of not taking a stand. When and how you Take a Stand is likewise important to assure that your voice and actions are most likely to bring positive results.

Leaders in any field must know when and how to stand up against injustice, discrimination, and unethical behavior with wisdom and decisiveness if we are to build workplaces and communities where everyone has a fair opportunity to flourish and prosper.

WHAT DOES IT MEAN TO "TAKE A STAND"?

Mistakes. Misunderstandings. Prejudice. Thoughtlessness.

All of us have cultural biases and blind spots shaped by our upbringing and experiences that influence the attitudes, words, and behaviors we accept and those to which we object.

When you Take a Stand and call out attitudes and behaviors that represent any form of microaggression, belittling, bullying, bias, or discrimination, even if they're not directed against you personally, you help weed out those attitudes and behaviors. Sadly, there will be those who Take a Stand to defend the status quo, even if it means support-ing inequity or continuing to institutionalize discrimination and bias. When you Take a Stand, I encourage you to ask yourself questions like these: Will my words or action help to enable another person or group to be treated equitably and with respect, just as I would want to be treated if I were in their place? Do I need to speak up for myself because I am not being treated fairly or respectfully? Is there injustice or inhu-manity that needs to be called out or prevented? This book is not designed to help you determine what's right versus wrong. That would take a lot more than I have the capacity to offer. The point is to encourage you to Take Stock of your values and beliefs to Take a Stand when you feel they have been violated or crossed.

> **Take Stock of your values and beliefs to Take a Stand when you feel they have been violated or crossed.**

The particular boundaries and issues that trigger us to Take a Stand will shift over time, and they also vary with experience, so we need to be tactful, use good judgment, and be prepared to handle conflict constructively. Many professional women have experienced the sting of being mistaken for a subordinate male's assistant. A woman walks into a meeting with a junior male colleague, and those they are meeting with assume the junior male is the woman's superior. That's not a mistake a professional woman can allow to go uncorrected. But there's a lot of latitude in how to go about doing so. Some might use humor: "I haven't been the junior accountant in about twenty years, so I suppose my youthful appearance deceived you." Others might be more direct: "Joe is actually a member of my team." Yet another approach strikes a middle ground by using introductions with titles at the start of the meeting to correct the mistake. By correcting their error, you are taking a stand and speaking up for yourself as the senior professional to claim your "place" at the table. But how you correct the error must employ tact and not seek to unnecessarily embarrass the mistaken party. That's good advice to follow anytime you Take a Stand.

Even today, when people sometimes zero in on a physical attribute and comment on that repeatedly, any objection can be cast as a matter of oversensitivity, in a way that ignores the cumulative impact of such remarks. One of my friends has bright-red hair. I've lost count of the times I've heard people comment on her hair and ask if she has a flaming temper to match her flaming red hair. Most of these people are either casual acquaintances or have just been introduced to her, and it always strikes me as a cheap, tacky attempt at humor. As I know how it bothers my friend, sometimes I'll speak up so she doesn't have to and joke that it's my temper they ought to watch. My friend also developed her own fast replies over time, like, "Please don't quit your day job for comedy." Whether it's someone teasing about your weight, commenting on the texture of your hair or lack of it, or any other barb, you do not have to simply grin and bear it. If someone hurts or offends, you owe it to yourself to speak up, and depending on the situation, the best approach might be to take the person to the side privately.

I consider Take a Stand to be a constructive process that has the intent of initiating positive change, not a personal attack that involves bullying or threatening or worse, even if that's what you may have experienced and wish to respond. In the story that opens this chapter, I was angry and outraged by the blackface invitation and had no intention of accepting it, or letting the occasion pass by, but I didn't let my first response dictate my actions. My intention was not only to decline but also to be constructive, to point out the mistake and provide a chance to learn and apologize, not merely to admonish. Through my RSVP in this situation, I focused on letting them know

1. that blackface and minstrel shows were racially offensive (not just an event I had no interest in attending);

2. why Black people found that image offensive and racist (its roots in bigotry, oppression, and discrimination); and

3. that diverse views matter, and it's important to look at things from another's perspective and respect their opinions—even more importantly, to include diverse voices at the table.

Had I simply been angry but not spoken up, I would not have had the opportunity to help the company look more closely at future events and institutions they sponsored to apply a broader lens before attaching the company's name as a sponsor.

IT IS TIME FOR YOU TO TAKE A STAND WHEN ...

It is never wise to allow anyone to disrespect your talent and ability or diminish your light. That's a time when you have no choice but to stand up for yourself.

My sister, Vicki, has done so many things well over the years— film and television actress, music video producer, honors graduate from law school, big-firm associate, Peace Corps volunteer, pastry chef, schoolteacher—that her adaptability and resilience are traits that I both admire and from which I draw inspiration. For the past several years, she has enjoyed being the theater and drama teacher at international schools in Vietnam, China, Singapore, Egypt, and India, sharing her love of the theater arts with hundreds of children.

It is never wise to allow anyone to disrespect your talent and ability or diminish your light. That's a time when you have no choice but to stand up for yourself.

One area that she has been most focused on challenging is the lack of diverse perspectives in the curriculum offered by the international schools where she has taught. Most international schools profess in their mission statements a desire to promote an international mindset, encourage respect for cultural differences, and make the world a better place, but often in delivering the curriculum there is an overwhelming lack of inclusion of diverse perspectives beyond an Anglo-European viewpoint. As issues arise, Vicki does not hesitate to challenge the status quo and redesign learning engagements to include theater genres and styles from diverse cultures, spotlight non-Western writers and playwrights, and encourage students to attend and explore theatrical performances that celebrate other cultures. Challenging expat teachers and school administrators to cast off their arrogance that the Western perspective is superior and to be more respectful of the culture of their host nation is a constant struggle, as well as speaking up to recognize the local teachers whose contributions to the school are as dedicated, smart, and meaningful as the teachers who hail from Australia, New Zealand, Britain, Europe, Canada, and the United States but for whom that acknowledgment is harder won.

When the principal at one international school decided to cut the budget for a host culture week celebration that centered on an important national religious holiday because it was "a food/flags situation—not aligned to the IB philosophy," my sister raised her voice in objection. By challenging the disrespectful words and hypocrisy of the school's principal, which conflicted with the mission of the school to develop internationally minded students with respect for the views, cultures, values, and traditions of others, Vicki took a stand and found allies among the faculty, who were grateful to have her express what so many were thinking.

I firmly believe that whenever you encounter behaviors or attitudes that demean or discriminate against others, you should take a strong stand, whether the victim of that discrimination is yourself or someone else. The examples and issues that I am presenting here are not exhaustive, but they are intended to help you think about the many ways that you can stand up for others and support them. As a person who has been on the receiving end of discrimination since childhood, I cannot tell you how encouraging it is when someone comes alongside me and stands with me, and I have always tried to provide that same moral and practical support to others, both personally and at the level of institutional policy.

Sometimes, Take a Stand happens quietly and uses humor; at other times you need to be direct. I'll never forget the moment at a leadership retreat where we were all asked to share something about a personal preference or boundary that our colleagues should be advised not to cross. When it was my turn, I said that for me, the N-word was a fighting word and if anyone used it in my presence or directed it at me, I would take them up on it. After a moment's silence, my boss responded to my words and tone with, "Well, if anyone wants to pick that fight with Veta, you've been warned," which had the effect of emphasizing my boundary and letting it be known he would not tolerate it either.

POLICIES AND PRACTICES

During my days at Sunoco in an era before everyone had their own mobile phone, a managerial directive was issued regarding the development of a new policy on the use of work phones to make private/personal phone calls. The new phone policy had been formulated by a managerial committee comprised solely of men who were married with children. Their new policy stated employees were permitted to use the company's phone only to call a spouse or children, or to make calls about the medical or educational needs of the employee and their spouse or children. The policy effectively barred single, childless employees from using the company phone for any purpose except their own medical or academic needs. Everyone with responsibilities for parents, siblings, or partners was out of luck. Although not developed with malicious intent, the policy was simply insufficiently thought through, because the group that developed it had one narrow perspective and experience. The policy was quickly updated when employees pointed out the limitations it represented. But getting that policy changed meant that people had to speak up and point out the problems. They did, and it was.

While phone policies are not such an issue these days, you may encounter other issues that are—perhaps it may be policies that do not reflect the needs of a diverse workforce, like promotion practices based on tenure instead of merit, inconsistent approaches to overtime pay, failure to widely publicize open positions, and the like, against which you need to Take a Stand. But taking a stand is more than just objecting to what's wrong and waiting for the "powers that be" to address it for you. How often are there opportunities for you to contribute toward creating policies that "do right"? There's a big difference between taking a stand and simply being a complainer. Instead of sitting back, criticizing, and waiting for "management" to address something in your workplace, why not constructively raise the issue or problem and suggest how it might be addressed or solved? The world is full of complainers who sit on the sidelines squawking about what others are not doing for them. But there are too few people willing to step up, to Take a Stand, to demonstrate initiative, and to make a positive difference in their workplaces, neighborhoods, and communities.

> **The world is full of complainers who sit on the sidelines squawking about what others are not doing for them.**

CASUAL CONVERSATIONS

I believe discrimination is often more prevalent at a social level than it is at a policy level because these days, lawyers and risk managers often check policies and public statements to protect organizations and executives from litigation based upon claims of discrimination. But conversations in cafeterias, grocery stores, living rooms, and offices do not have the same level of oversight and censorship. If you are the recipient of derogatory or offensive comments, or if you overhear someone else making those types of comments and let the moment pass without speaking up, you are empowering the belief that such speech is acceptable. It's a moment when you will be tested to Take a Stand. You don't need to be confrontational about it; I have discovered that an "Ouch, that hurts!" response often attracts an apology and an opportunity for dialogue. The comment **may** have been habitual or unthinking, but that is part of the problem. If you don't call it out, you are enabling the offense and preventing the other person from taking the chance to reexamine their beliefs and their language because someone they know and respect called it out.

Depending upon the nature of the conversation and your relationship with the parties, it may be preferable to wait until there's a private opportunity to "take your stand" and use it as an opportunity to educate or inform. I think it's always best to assume that no one wants to intentionally offend another person, and I have found most offensive comments or actions are born of ignorance and underexposure to diverse people and experiences.

> I think it's always best to assume that no one wants to intentionally offend another person, and I have found most offensive comments or actions are born of ignorance and underexposure to diverse people and experiences.

Perhaps you have experienced someone who made assumptions that you would not be interested in taking on management of a project. This could be the result of their misperceptions that you always seem to be busy, or you have after-work care responsibilities for a loved one, or you just started grad school, so that's a reason not to ask you. If you suspect others' limitations on how they look at your situation or what they think you can handle have resulted in your being passed over for developmental opportunities, be sure to clarify your availability and interest. In this instance, Take a Stand means speaking up to clarify your desire to be considered or to volunteer.

PHYSICAL AND MENTAL DISABILITIES

The assumptions we make about people who use assistive devices can be breathtakingly insensitive. Here in the West, we no longer shut people out of sight because they have mental or physical challenges, but we could do a lot more to make our workforces and our communities a lot more accessible and welcoming.

It is not so very long ago that public buildings did not need to have wheelchair access or accommodations for people with disabilities, and even now, many older "historical sites" remain hard for many to navigate. At different times, I have seen people talking over the head of someone in a wheelchair or rushing ahead of them on the Metro as though they were barriers to press past, or I have observed someone speak for a blind person with a cane as though the person could not hear or answer for herself. I would encourage all of us to take time to educate ourselves regarding the experiences of people with disabilities. Awareness increases empathy and informs us how to treat others respectfully, with dignity and value. If you happen to have a disability, please do not hesitate to let others know when their offers to help may be unwelcome or unnecessary. Also, please do not hesitate to educate your colleagues, neighbors, and friends regarding your disability and how they can be supportive.

Fortunately, mental health issues are receiving a lot more attention, especially as we have all struggled under the weight of the pandemic and being socially distant. Yet the attention has not dispelled many of the stigmas that sometimes attach to mental disabilities and mental illness. Wellness programs and initiatives have become more important than ever. You can take a positive stand in support of your colleagues and your own mental and intellectual health by engaging in activities and programs designed to foster a healthy, balanced approach to work, home, and personal responsibilities.

RACE, GENDER, AND SEXUAL ORIENTATION

These are some of the hot-button issues of our day, and while we have made progress, we still too often hear derogatory comments and dismissive actions that diminish a person's value because of these characteristics. Too many people continue to be mistreated, discriminated against, even persecuted and killed because of their race, gender, or sexual orientation, and biases, both conscious and unconscious, result in diminished opportunities.

When George Floyd was killed by a Minneapolis police officer who pressed his knee on the neck of the unarmed and restrained Black man for almost nine minutes as George Floyd pleaded for mercy to just breathe, the callousness and lack of humanity by a police officer sworn to protect and to serve triggered worldwide protest and cries for racial justice. That tragic death sparked a number of conversations about the injustices Black and Brown people face. Many listened as friends, neighbors, colleagues, and family members shared the indignities and discrimination they experience all too often. In this instance, standing up meant Black and Brown people being courageous enough to share their stories, and people who weren't Black or Brown speaking up to say Black Lives Matter and then supporting opportunities to demonstrate that they do. And as many Asian people have been scorned during the pandemic, attacked, and accused of causing what some ignorantly labeled the "China virus," I believe Take a Stand means calling out and opposing that sort of bigotry.

Whether it's speaking up for working parents to be offered a bit more flexibility as they grapple with homeschooling, remote work, and demanding responsibilities, or supporting a transgender colleague to get coworkers to use the correct pronoun, that's taking a stand.

Within the past school year, a lawyer I have known for more than ten years posted to social media about the frustration he experienced at his child's school, where permission slips still had two lines for parents' names labeled "mother" and "father." Well, this lawyer and his husband were constantly having to correct the form, and it was frustrating. Even the limitation of two lines for parents ignores the many single-parent and stepfamily relationships resulting from divorce. How nice it would have been if other parents had spoken up to tell the school that the form did not reflect today's diverse families and should be revised to say "parent(s)."

PERSONAL ISSUES AND ACCOMMODATIONS

Taking a stand doesn't need to be confrontational; it can simply be a way of negotiating an outcome that meets the needs of two parties, as Victor discovered when he was accepted to law school. Victor was an outstanding employee whose hard work and team spirit made him popular with customers and colleagues. After being accepted to law school, Victor went to management and asked whether he could continue to work full time for the organization while he studied to become a lawyer. He did a wonderful job of preparing his case, framing it as part of his overall life plan, and detailing how he could go to law school part time in the evening while fulfilling his full-time responsibilities as well as bring additional value to his work. Victor's plan included the work-schedule accommodations he would need, as well as a request to take leave from ACC over the summer to gain legal experience outside our organization. If he had needed to so do, I'm sure Victor would have been ready to remind his manager of the many contributions he had made over the years, but we were well aware of those and happy to agree to his requests and approve the necessary accommodations.

Victor advocated for himself, after applying many other habits discussed in this book—he had taken stock, was stepping out of the status quo to Take Risk, and was prepared to Take Credit to cite his contributions, although ultimately that wasn't necessary. Victor is now in-house counsel at a large telecommunications company, where he is steadily progressing in knowledge and responsibility and was recently promoted. But that career path would never have happened for him if Victor had not spoken up for himself and his best interests.

CONTRIBUTIONS

I think it's important to focus on the idea of contribution to society and increasing representation. As a Black female, I probably would not have enjoyed the opportunities I have had others not paved the way before me and given me a hand when I needed it. That is why I am an advocate for joining networks and organizations to support people from specific underrepresented groups such as racial/ethnic minorities, women, LGBTQ+, people with disabilities, et cetera. You do not have to be a member of a particular group to support and advocate for them and Take a Stand for the issues important to their equality and inclusion. It's one of the reasons I especially enjoy mentoring younger professionals who share my demographic traits as well as those who do not. Forming relationships with people who are different may take a bit more effort, but it's well worth it. So if you are not investing in someone who could use your help, Take a Stand for next-generation leaders, and support their growth!

> If you are not investing in someone who could use your help, Take a Stand for next-generation leaders, and support their growth!

THE COST OF TAKING A STAND

At one stage, I was appointed to a leadership council that was dedicated to exploring ways in which lawyers could provide a greater benefit to society by advancing diversity and pro bono service. Among the subjects we explored was the way in which in-house counsel at corporations could move the needle on inclusion of racial/ethnic minorities, women, and LGBTQ+ people by being more strident about the diversity of the law firms they retained as outside counsel. We spent hours discussing and formulating our statements in various groups and put forward some noble aspirational statements about what we wanted to see, but the group hesitated about actually including requirements for change. I was increasingly concerned as I saw the opportunity to create real change slipping away and wrote an advocacy statement on why we, as a group, needed to take a strong stand on this and include metrics and goals that would be measured against annually if we genuinely wanted to spur progress. For me, this was an imperative step forward in the commitment to advance diversity and inclusion. We needed more than merely a "nice-to-have" statement that would make us feel as though we were doing something. It was time to advance from feeling good to doing good and achieving results.

From working in a corporation, I knew that what's valued is measured, so without clearly defined metrics against which to measure progress, the effort wouldn't be worth the paper the aspirational statements were printed on. My advocacy proved instrumental in turning the opinion of the council members toward more assertive expectations, and one of its members was so upset that her more conservative recommendation had lost out that she reported my actions to my boss at the time, alleging I had gone too far. My boss then came to me and asked what was going on and whether there might be a way forward that didn't make people like that woman feel so uncomfortable.

I explained to him that that was the crux of the diversity debate. As long as everyone was focused on feeling comfortable, then change would be impossible, and diversity would continue to languish. I said that I regretted the woman who complained felt upset about the result, but I was pleased that I had eloquently expressed my opinion and won my point with the group, so I did not feel sorry for making anyone feel uncomfortable, and in good faith, I could not apologize for the stand I took. I reminded my boss that having a diverse staff meant that I might see and advocate differently on issues like this.

What I didn't say directly in that moment was that for me, this was a line in the sand. I was prepared to pay the price for my advocacy, even if that meant that I would need to resign from the organization if it came to that. I really did not care about making anyone feel uncomfortable if their comfort required that I support the status quo or walk back what I said. Ultimately, my boss agreed that we were following a path that was in line with our organization's values, and I earned his respect for standing up on behalf of my principles, even if it created short-term discomfort and tension with some members of the group.

My biggest learning from that moment is that discomfort is the price we pay for any type of change, especially social and economic change. If you believe that what you are saying or doing is right and your goal is to create opportunities and remove barriers for people who are overlooked or discriminated against, then it doesn't matter how uncomfortable it may be; you need to summon your voice and speak out to Take a Stand. By doing so, you create the potential to connect with allies and supporters, and by joining together you will cover more ground and help move the needle of progress.

When you Take a Stand, it sometimes comes with a cost, so be sure you think that through. For example, when my sister challenged the principal at her school for being disrespectful of another culture, she took the risk that she could be reprimanded or fired, yet it was important to her to speak up nonetheless. Before you stick your neck out, it is important to reflect carefully and consider whether you are willing to pay the potential price. Once you've raised an issue and committed yourself, it may be too late to undo your actions. Thus, two useful questions to ask yourself are the following:

- Can I live with the consequences of this action if I Take a Stand and things don't go well?

- Can I live with myself if I **don't** stand up for this cause or position that reflects my values?

Let your answers to these two questions guide whether and how you Take a Stand or live with the consequences of choosing not to do so. And remember the other habits that will help you assess what you should do, especially to Take Stock and reach out to others for a hand and advice.

THE ORGANIZATIONAL BENEFITS OF DIVERSITY

Studies have demonstrated that diversity benefits organizations as well as individuals by delivering more effective solutions to problems, in addition to stimulating creativity, adaptability, and innovation.[20] Sometimes, people complain that it takes longer to arrive at solutions when you are looking at an issue from a variety of perspectives, but this is to confuse efficiency with effectiveness. It may be quicker and more **efficient** to arrive at a decision when you have a homogenous group of decision makers, but the final decision is usually more **effective** when you have a diverse group of perspectives weighing in.

As a leader and someone who is called upon to solve problems and manage people daily, I want people around me who speak up, **especially** if they disagree with the majority view, because that divergent perspective can be a source of greater innovation or solutions that stand the test of time. I believe that both society and organizations benefit from appropriately expressed dissent, so you are shortchanging your organization if you stay silent, even if speaking leads to some uncomfortable interactions.

One woman told me the story of sitting as a new member on a board of directors for several sessions and listening to them trying to solve an issue but feeling too intimidated to speak out about a major oversight she had observed. Her rationale was, "It was so obvious that I knew they must have already considered its implications and decided it wasn't relevant." When she finally mentioned the issue, there was a stunned silence around the table. No one had thought of that perspective at all! It takes a range of voices to create full harmony, and disagreement is an important tool for solidifying your own opinions and adapting your thinking to include new possibilities.

---

20   Terry L. Howard, Evan A. Peterson, and Gregory W. Ulferts, "A Note on the Value of Diversity in Organizations," *International Journal of Management and Decision Making* 16, no. 3, (2017): 187; Deborah Hicks-Clarke and Paul Iles, "Climate for Diversity and Its Effects on Career and Organisational Attitudes and Perceptions," *Personnel Review* 29, no. 3 (2000): 324-45.

HOW TO TAKE A STAND

When you Take a Stand in the workplace, it can be very intimidating. You will have to combat your fear about the career implications of your action, especially if you are in a fairly conservative profession such as medicine, finance, or law. The dangers of this are real, but sometimes it's the only thing you can do, not only for yourself, but also for the wider community. Whenever you are tempted to stay silent and accept injustice or suppress your life goals or core values just to stay "safe," think about what that will do to your own soul and how it will affect the people who look to you as a model.

Once you have decided to Take a Stand, there are some elements that you need to consider:

- How important is this outcome to me?

- What specifically is important about this issue?

- What does success look like for taking a stand on this issue; what is the desired outcome?

- How will I get what I need to succeed?

- What price am I willing to pay to get this outcome?

- What mental and physical toll will I suffer from choosing to sit silent?

- Who are the allies that can support me in this effort?

Finding allies and supporters is extremely important. This was part of my strategy when I wanted to persuade the leadership council that our statement about diversity would not be complete without clearly defined goals and targets. I knew that my voice alone would not be sufficient, so I reviewed the issues and wrote a persuasive paper that swayed a majority of my peers.

Sometimes, your ally might be an organization that advocates on behalf of its members or to further a mission.

When I took leadership of MCCA, the organization's mission was advancing diversity in the legal profession, but the association defined that very narrowly to include just gender and race/ethnicity, but it was clear that there were other issues and underrepresented groups (LGBTQ+, people with disabilities, generational groups) that fell within our mandate. Rather than asking the MCCA board for permission, I decided to expand the mission to address a broader mandate and apologize later if the board objected. In addition to finding companies and individuals that wanted to work with us, we also looked for others who had successfully addressed these challenges that we could use as models. I also noticed that unlike every other gathering of lawyers, MCCA's gatherings had very few White men in attendance. When I asked White men whom I had known and worked with for years why they did not come to MCCA's events, they spoke candidly about how they did not feel like they belonged at a diversity event. How weird it sounded for anyone to feel excluded when the whole point of diversity programs is to spur greater inclusion!

Some of my colleagues were skeptical when I reached out to White males and invited them to speak at diversity events and contribute their perspectives, too, but I knew that the most insightful advice often comes from people who are already "insiders," and we certainly need inside help if we hope that things will change. In fact, one of the strategies that we developed was an awards program to recognize leaders in this field. That first year the winner of the law firm award was a Midwest law firm that was among the first in the United States to stand for LGBTQ+ inclusion, and they did so from a deeply conservative part of the country. John Murphy, then the firm's managing partner, is a straight, White, male lawyer who spearheaded the initiative out of respect for the rights and autonomy of others, including people who were different from himself. This attitude is what we need to foster: the sense that we are not only taking a stand on behalf of our own community but also supporting our shared humanity in all its diversity, speaking and acting consistently and as persuasively and strategically as possible. As I got to know John, he shared his own story of having to advocate in support of his son, Jack, who has Down syndrome. John understood the sting of people lowering expectations and thus the types of opportunities that Jack would receive. Well, John eventually retired from practicing law to work as a diversity consultant to help other organizations find their way to stronger D&I programs, and Jack went on to attend college.

RESPONDING CONSTRUCTIVELY WHEN SOMEONE TAKES A STAND

Just as the manner in which you Take a Stand will influence your effectiveness in reaching your goals, the manner in which you respond when someone takes a stand against you is critical. Mostly people fail to achieve their goals when they are loud, indignant, self-righteous, or bullying and try to intimidate others, so you need to find a better way forward, a way that leaves them open to different perspectives and new ways of thinking and acting.

If you yell at someone and tell them how insensitive and ignorant they are, there is a high probability that they will yell back, and the conflict and disagreement will escalate, whereas a lighter touch might open the door to an apology and discussion.

Shortly after the state of California passed legislation mandating that there would be a quota for the number of women serving on the boards of public companies, I was talking to one of our sponsors about it. This man's firm is a very generous donor to our organization, and a person whom I greatly respect, and he said to me, "Veta, I don't understand why diversity efforts have moved toward quotas. What's your view on quotas?"

Expedience may have suggested that I should fudge my views under the circumstances, but I couldn't do that, so I looked him straight in the eye and responded with reason: "You know, it seems to me that we've been at this a long time, and there are a lot of studies that show what women bring to the table, but we just don't seem to be getting the numbers, even though we both know many highly qualified women. So maybe it's time to try something new and be a bit more purposeful about it." He then nodded his head after reflecting on my opinion, and we continued to enjoy a nice lunch, exchanging news about people we knew in common and discussing opportunities for our organizations to deepen the relationship.

> **When you are taking a stand on a topic that may prove controversial, finding a thought-provoking response will reduce tension, deescalate a situation, and potentially eliminate any embarrassment if they decide they are on the wrong side (i.e., not yours!) of the debate.**

When you are taking a stand on a topic that may prove controversial, finding a thought-provoking response will reduce tension, deescalate a situation, and potentially eliminate any embarrassment if they decide they are on the wrong side (i.e., not yours!) of the debate. Here are some possible responses you could use to do that graciously:

- What is your view on ... ? (Invites the other person to share their perspective.)

- I'm curious whether you have considered ... ? (Offers a different perspective on the situation or issue.)

- I wonder how that will help us to... ? (Reminds them of your shared goal.)

- Have you seen this research ... ? (Lets them know that they might not have all the information.)

- Ouch, that hurt! (When your colleague makes a statement that is hurtful, let them know. It opens the door for an apology and an opportunity to learn and understand why you found their comment objectionable.)

I quite enjoy this process, which makes taking a stand and advocating like a mental chess match ... an intellectually challenging undertaking that entails strategy and carefully planned countermoves to advance your position. When you win agreement or bend someone's view toward your own, victory is much sweeter than if you win simply by being the loudest voice in the room.

My goal when I challenge someone who holds views that oppose mine is that they will respect me as a person of credibility and substance, even if they don't agree with me. As I give the best possible response that I can, it is my ambition to shake the biases and paradigms that may have been planted by society. You can do that, too, as you learn to disarm someone's instinctive, fear-based response to change by questioning their closely held beliefs with graciousness, quick wit, and courage.

I am deeply concerned about the stridency and incivility that people now employ in any debate because I believe the increasing levels of societal anger and violence stoke the fires of fear, undermine democracy, and inhibit progress rather than giving it momentum. It's important to remember this as you confront personal and social issues that need to be resolved. We can't turn back the pages of history, and I am eternally grateful for the men and women who gave their lives to abolish slavery in the United States so that I now enjoy the freedoms that I have today. It took a civil war and a lot of bloodshed to secure that freedom, but it was followed by bitterness, destruction, and Jim Crow. I wish I felt more confident that our nation has learned a lesson and that the pathway to full equality for African Americans, Black, Brown, Asian, and other racial/ethnic minorities will be achieved cooperatively and respectfully. For the equally critical racial justice issues of our day, I'd like to find that better way.

NOW IT'S YOUR TURN ...

Every era offers an opportunity to create massive positive change, but this is the moment that you have been given to step up and raise your voice on behalf of others. What are you going to do about your opportunity?

Will you be ready to grasp hold of this moment and speak out consistently with your values ... or will you let it slip away through fear, lack of observation, or lack of ability to persuade and influence others?

Now that you've learned the importance of stepping out of your comfort zone to Take a Stand, it's time to move on to the subject of leadership, or the next essential habit, Take Command ...

IN CHAPTER 6 YOU LEARNED:

- Take a Stand is an essential habit that becomes an expression of your core values and is something we all should be prepared to do.

- Sometimes it is more important to speak out than to hide in comfortable silence and ignorance.
- Take a Stand is not just about defending your own interests; you can (and should) also Take a Stand on behalf of others who are in need of an advocate.
- Diversity is a strength that leads to greater innovation and more effective problem solving, which is needed more than ever in a world where disruption is becoming the norm.
- Take a Stand comes with a price tag, and you may need to be prepared to pay it if necessary.
- If done appropriately, Take a Stand can lead to constructive dialogue.
- Solutions only come when you are willing to sit with people who disagree with you and be uncomfortable.

TAKE SIX

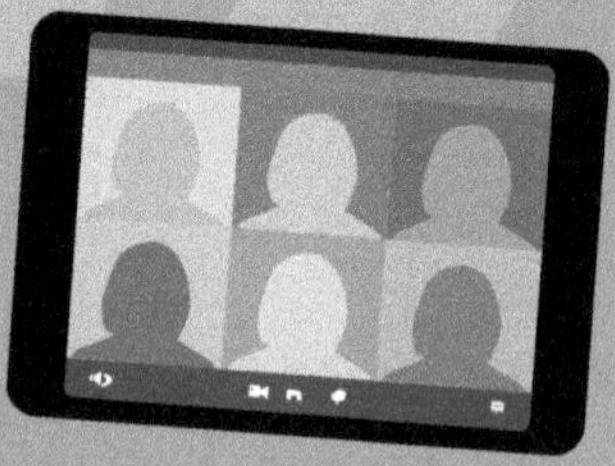

CHAPTER SEVEN

TAKE
COMMAND

You never have to ask anyone's permission to lead. Just lead!

—KAMALA HARRIS

On Tuesday, October 23, 2001, I stood at the podium and looked out at the crowded room of men and women in tuxedos and gowns. My heart was full of gratitude for their presence and support for the work of MCCA, despite the recent tragedy. The memory of those who should have been there with us haunted me and stiffened my conviction that holding the event was a fitting tribute to them.

Hotel staff hovered around the edges of the room, and I thanked them as well. Many of those present were grieving for family, friends, and colleagues, as they walked around a city that had so recently shifted from peaceful prosperity and innocence to devastation and the aftermath of profoundly evil acts.

In the midst of great darkness and personal tragedy, each person in that room was there to Take Command of the future. They were there to affirm their commitment to American values, rebuilding New York, and creating hope, and to honor the belief that everyone has a right to life, liberty, and the pursuit of happiness and that their support of MCCA helped ensure those rights were extended to diverse, under-represented groups.

I took over at MCCA in January 2001. Never could I have imagined how my first year leading any organization would bring challenges that would redefine and reshape who I am, teach me lifelong lessons about how to lead, and strengthen my commitment to making a positive difference in this world.

My first weeks—as I've mentioned—were chaotic. The small nonprofit organization was about $900,000 in debt, and we had to draw from a line of credit to meet payroll. There was a real possibility that we could be forced to close and abandon our efforts to open up pathways for underrepresented minority groups within the legal profession. Our focus throughout that year was on preparing for a big educational conference and massive fundraising dinner to be held in New York City, the corporate heart of the United States, on Tuesday, October 23, 2001. We had booked the biggest hotel ballroom in New York City with the expectation of hosting one thousand–plus people and raising more than half a million dollars in donations, tickets, and pledges so that we could continue clawing our way back to financial stability. If we failed, our survival was doubtful. At the very best, failure would trigger more debt, and if we survived, our potential for real impact would certainly be reduced to virtual insignificance ... and with it my reputation as an effective CEO.

Soon after 8:46 a.m. on September 11, the radio program I was listening to as I drove to work was interrupted by news of the American Airlines plane striking the north tower of the World Trade Center in New York City. As I was approaching my office in Washington, DC, I heard the news of a second plane striking the World Trade Center as well as reports of an attack on the Pentagon, and it was clear that these were no random accidents. The thought that was uppermost in my mind was, "America is under attack, and we are at war!" I felt I needed to warn my colleagues at MCCA and the law firm that provided our office space. So I drove into the underground car park and leaped out of my car. Handing the keys to the attendant, I said, "Don't park my car; I won't be staying. We're at war, and the Pentagon was just attacked."

I ran up three flights of stairs to the offices we shared with the law firm and ran around the third floor of the office suite shouting, "America is at war! Evacuate the city! Go home!"

Everyone was hard at work. Some people looked up and frowned at my disturbance. A few people ignored me completely. One or two got up and shut their office doors so they could get on with their important work. Deflated and breathless, I went over to MCCA's section of the office suite and told all the MCCA staff to pack up their things, go home immediately, and text me when they had arrived safely. At that moment, work was secondary to safety. I waited while all the MCCA staff packed up, and we walked out together so everyone could head home.

By the time the official announcement to evacuate Washington, DC, was made, the MCCA employees and I were all safely home watching with horror the images of the Twin Towers collapse and learning of the crash of a fourth plane into a field in Pennsylvania.

Later, as we watched the chaos on the DC area roads and public transportation, we were so glad we had acted quickly and decisively, as many of those who waited to leave the city were stranded for hours on the crowded roads and public transport.

Over the next hours and days, I watched in disbelief as the facts began to unfold and heard the news of the human toll in New York City, in Pennsylvania, and at the Pentagon. Our professional network included hundreds of people who worked in the NYC financial district, World Trade Center buildings, and the Pentagon. Two questions buzzed in my mind: "Where are they now?" and "What will happen next?"

I was guiltily aware of another, even more personal, consideration lurking behind those questions: "What about MCCA's fundraiser and future?" It seemed selfish to think about it while we watched and waited and grieved, but the issue was looming nevertheless. MCCA was my immediate responsibility, and I would need to make a decision about the fundraising event quickly. I couldn't just wait, hope, and see how things developed.

Our team talked about the most appropriate response in endless circles. We quickly realized that there was no right answer and just as many valid reasons to cancel as there were to continue.

In the end, I made the decision to go ahead with the event. It was true that we couldn't afford not to, but there was a deeper reason: my desire to take hold of the moment and to hold up a beacon of hope as we advanced a mission that mattered.

I prepared a carefully scripted message and sat up late every evening to call the list of MCCA supporters in NYC and beyond, after hours so I wouldn't have to speak to anyone in person and make them feel obligated to accept. I was embarrassed and ashamed to ask people to show up for a dinner so soon after such a massive tragedy, yet I believed it was also a fitting tribute to those who perished—to prevent terrorism from taking more from us than it already had. Some of MCCA's biggest supporters had offices in and around the World Trade Center, and they were decimated. Our community had lost friends, colleagues, loved ones in this world-changing tragedy.

Over and over, I left the message that I hoped would convey my understanding if they felt unable to support us at this event, my own sense of grief and sympathy, and MCCA's desperate struggle for survival so that it could continue its work of creating a better future, which was the impetus for my decision to move forward.

There were plenty of voices saying, "You can't expect anyone to show up. Just cancel it, and give people a chance to grieve."

I heard them.

I also heard the voices that said, "There are so many dark forces that we can't overcome and lives we can't bring back. Here is a chance to stand for the values we all share and offer hope."

The latter were the voices I clung to, and I had some kind of affirmation from the many people who attended despite everything, from others who sent their well wishes, from the hotel staff who were grateful for the work, and for the glimmer of hope for a "new normal."

IT'S TIME TO TAKE COMMAND

Mahatma Gandhi famously said, "A small body of determined spirits fired by an unquenchable faith in their mission can alter the course of history." He believed that this applied not only to his nation's political independence but also to the social and political evils he saw around him, and that change started with individuals.

As the chief executive of MCCA, I knew the decision to hold or cancel our most important annual fundraiser ultimately fell on my shoulders. I drew on all the principles we've already explored as I

- took stock of my options and weighed the consequences and needs from all sides;

- evaluated the risks that each path entailed for the organization and my own reputation as a leader;

- mentally tallied up my actions and responses from the past and took credit for past positive outcomes to bolster confidence in my decision and positive influence MCCA had made and hoped to continue making;

- sought advice from others and then took the help they offered, not trying to do it all myself;

- actively invited opinions and critique from everyone at the table so that we could see the risks, dangers, and rewards as clearly as possible;

- determined the path we would take and took a stand to defend that decision and resist the temptation to waver; and

- took command and led our team to made it happen.

From the perspective of practical activity and logistics, my contribution to the event was relatively minor, but as a leader my role represented the difference between success and failure. The event proved a fundraising success, raising more than we dared to hope, and MCCA paid off all its debts, going on to become a real force in the legal profession.

WHAT DOES IT MEAN TO TAKE COMMAND?

A true leader leads because he or she has a compelling vision and a plan of execution, which they pursue unapologetically and inspire other people to follow. Have you ever noticed that some people who are appointed to lead organizations or those who are elected to an office can be professionally competent and even good at taking a stand, yet inadequate when it comes to Take Command? For me, that failure to Take Command is especially disappointing in the case of women leaders because too few of us achieve the top spot.

It mystified me for a long time why Teresa May was such a successful leader when she was in Opposition yet crumbled when she became Prime Minister. As I was reflecting on the idea of taking command, I realized

> A true leader leads because he or she has a compelling vision and a plan of execution, which they pursue unapologetically and inspire other people to follow.

that when May was leading the Opposition, she was extremely good at taking a stand (mostly against the government) and mustering support to resist them. However, when she was elevated to a top spot in government, she needed to be decisive, have a vision, and Take Command, which was not a skill that she had practiced. She fell into a trap that I've seen in others who work so hard to build consensus and to please everyone: ultimately, she undermined her authority and the confidence others had in her decisions and leadership.

Across the pond here in the United States, House Speaker Nancy Pelosi and the former Senate Majority Leader Mitch McConnell are both very visible examples of what Take Command can look like in practice and a source for some interesting reflections on the different standards for men and women. Although their beliefs and strategy are poles apart, regardless of what you may think of the positions they take, both of them communicate a clear vision and are comfortable demanding the respect and attention of their followers. Both politicians have virulent detractors as well, but they are focused, tenacious, and lead their political parties on clearly charted paths to ambitious goals. So what's different about their leadership styles as they accept being in command? Mitch leads unapologetically and, as a man, has no need to trot out his wife or children to demonstrate that he's really a caring, compassionate person. His family life is largely irrelevant to his leadership brand. In contrast, as a woman, Nancy is no less commanding, but she is expected to demonstrate qualities Mitch does not, so she is occasionally photographed with her children and grandchildren at the Capitol and shows a softer side. Both Nancy and Mitch have five-letter first names, but it's only Nancy who is too often referred to as a five-letter word that is not her given name—a derisive word that too often attaches to women leaders.

TAKING SITUATIONAL COMMAND

Maybe you don't see yourself as the kind of leader whose name is emblazoned across the opening pages of newspapers, so you've assumed that you don't need to Take Command. Think again.

Imagine that you are on a bus driving through the countryside and there is an accident. Someone has to take charge, or people will panic, and lives may be lost. Are you the kind of person who would stand up and say, "Follow me," and then help people off the bus, get them safely away, and take care of the injured? That's situational leadership.

During the 2020 pandemic, Brendan, a manager at a widely respected nonprofit association, stepped into this kind of command. The global uncertainty, general levels of fear and anxiety about the health and well-being of loved ones, plus the challenges of isolation, homeschooling, and working from home took a toll on people's mental health. Brendan didn't wait to be asked to lead; he was aware of the growing problem and had a keen interest in the subject because of his own background, so he instituted a weekly "Wellness Wednesday" briefing for all staff. Every Wednesday for several months, Brendan shared what he had learned about self-care through his own past journey out of an addiction and held out a shining vision of what wellness means to him. He knew that many of his team members might be too embarrassed to acknowledge their weakness and needs, so he shared his own story and struggles as well as practical strategies to give people a sense of reassurance, empathy, confidence, and hope. He earned the moniker "the Wellness Guy" for his dedication to helping his colleagues through a difficult time.

Brendan was not alone. There was also Pam, who works as a specialist at the same organization. She showed up to every virtual meeting during the pandemic, taking care to project professionally and positively. Pam sensed she had colleagues who might appreciate a little optimism each morning, so she began to share an inspirational message with her coworkers at the start of each workday. Brendan and Pam are terrific examples of situational leadership, which has less to do with job title or place in a hierarchy and more to do with their ability to sense a void and step into it with confidence. Leaders step up and they lead; they don't wait to be invited.

The 2020 pandemic provided many opportunities for people to step up and Take Command in the event and hospitality space as well. In some communities, restaurants took the initiative to set up mobile stations and feed overworked healthcare workers, first responders, and the homeless. This idea then spread to other communities, as many people chose to do whatever possible to encourage and support others through difficult times. Organizations around the world (including my own) consulted with event organizers and wrestled with decisions about what to do about their educational programs and conferences. In a normal year, these decisions are made by a talented team of professionals, as the projected number of attendees, speakers, and timeline for preparations is quite consistent from year to year, but the pandemic made everything topsy-turvy.

At the start of the COVID-19 shutdown in March 2020, we all assumed that in a few months, everything would be back to normal, but as the weeks passed, we wondered if that was a realistic expectation. Eventually, our team sat down and discussed possibilities, and I made the decision that we would let go of the belief that things would soon normalize and undertake plans to hold a 100 percent virtual event, despite having zero experience doing anything like that before. After my early decision, responsibility passed back to our education team to devise and execute the plan ... and the entire team stepped up and did an incredible job working together and sorting out all the technical and logistical solutions we needed, including having a subset of us devise backup plans and communications strategies in case we had equipment or internet failures. Hearing the stories about so many innovative and effective solutions people came up with reinforced my belief that there is an enormous quantity of untapped potential in every organization and community and nation. Imagine what would happen if we were all committed to exploring that potential within ourselves and in others without waiting to be asked.

TAKING INSTITUTIONAL COMMAND

While situational command is often something you step into, institutional or organizational command is something that you are hired, appointed, or elected to take on and therefore something for which you can prepare and practice, starting in small ways and steadily building to greater levels of responsibility. I believe that being a leader means that you will sometimes have to make unpopular calls, since choosing one course of action means you will have rejected another choice that others supported. The ability to communicate those decisions, both big and small, is an essential leadership skill that requires courage and conviction, especially in the face of criticism. I believe this is where many leaders—both men and women—fall into the trap of overseeking consensus and becoming a victim of "analysis paralysis." However, the more I thought about this subject, the more I realized that there is a dual standard in this area. When a male leader makes a decision without full agreement or is seen as opinionated and outspoken, they are often admired and followed as a "strong leader." By contrast, when a female leader expresses her opinions clearly and is outspoken, she is regularly called out as arrogant and obnoxious (or worse, renamed that five-letter name).

I have seen and experienced real-life examples of this dynamic firsthand. One CEO, whom I'll call Clare, was highly qualified for the position and had spoken up vociferously when she was a vice president. So many of us had very high expectations when she was appointed CEO of her organization. Suddenly, it seemed as though she had a personality change when she became responsible, accountable, and authorized to call the shots. Whereas previously she could voice her opinions, step back, and leave it to someone else to make the final decision, when it was her turn to lead, she started to need a lot of approval before moving forward with decisions. Prior to key meetings, she would consult with her predecessor, whose name was Tom; then, during meetings, she would invite everyone else's opinion before offering a tentative decision that she inevitably clinched with the phrase, "I also discussed this with Tom, who thinks that we should do X, so that is my decision, too, and we will do X." During her tenure as the leader, we noticed she had real discomfort with making the final call and spoke more about others' opinions than she did her own. There was collective relief and a complete lack of surprise that she didn't last very long in the role.

Contrast this with another of my leadership role models, Joan. Joan is a consensus builder, and she is the chair of a global board of directors who all share a common vision, so their debate is over means rather than ends. That doesn't mean that there isn't vigorous discussion during meetings and differences of opinion. Actually, Joan **invites** disagreement and contrary opinions and makes sure that everyone has a voice, with no single voice allowed to dominate. I suspect that she often goes into these meetings with a clear idea of where things will end, but she asks open-ended questions that enlarge the scope of discussion and encourages each person to share what is important to them about the issue at hand. She listens actively so that she can discern what is needed to move everyone onto the same page, and she mirrors what she hears to ensure that all contributors know that their contribution was heard as the discussions advance to a conclusion. Where there is difference of opinion, that is acknowledged, and the points made are respected so that even when she decides to go in a different direction, she explains the logic behind her choice. Although some may disagree with the choice, they appreciate the opportunity to speak and be heard, respect the process, and therefore support the final decision.

There will inevitably be times when leaders have to make unpopular decisions, and as a result, although it's wrong, some people will transfer their dislike of the decision into dislike of the leader. My mother taught me early that being popular is overrated—I suspect that was designed to reinforce the idea that being punctual, diligent, polite, neat, clean, and well dressed was my duty, no matter what everyone else was doing—but I'm grateful for the lesson. It is one that every leader needs to learn and keep in mind because there is often a difference between doing what a leader feels is right and following popular opinion. Another lesson that Mom taught me is that you can passionately disagree with someone but still respect them and their choices.

Newcomers at organizations sometimes worry that lively discussions among the leadership mean that the leaders do not get along with each other, when in reality that debate is simply a reflection of leaders being leaders and expressing their contrasting views. I recall many years ago being asked by one of the staff where I worked why the executive team fought so much and whether the organization was in difficulties. It was interesting explaining that what she saw as dissension, I viewed as a healthy part of the decision-making process. Over time, I have learned the importance of looking deeply at the issues and not taking anything for granted. As a leader I have learned the importance of disagreement and debate, and nothing frightens me more than when I bring a suggestion to the table and everyone immediately says, "What a great idea!" That's when I'll ask others to tell me what I've missed or what could go wrong, or ask them

> **You can passionately disagree with someone but still respect them and their choices.**

how it's similar or different to what we've done in the past. No leader can afford to surround herself with yes-people—you're asking for a very one-dimensional decision-making process.

Taking command in an organization of any size involves dealing with complex, multifaceted issues on which you should expect to hear contrary views. For example, in every organization grappling with balancing its annual budget, there are some fixed elements that need to be met, such as rent, utilities, programs, services, and salaries; then there is a question of the projected revenue from programs and services and the possibility of surplus. In most years, the fixed elements don't generate much discussion, but the investment of any surplus is frequently the subject of lively debate about value, needs, and ROI, and there are always going to be several good options from which priorities need to be determined and decisions need to be made. Ultimately boards and chief executives take responsibility for the decisions that must be made, but all of us know that our decisions might have to change and that our organization might have to pivot in the face of circumstances beyond our control. During the pandemic, for example, how many of us announced office reopening dates, only to reassess that as new information about the depth and breadth of the coronavirus kept unfolding?

Leadership is like that: you make a decision on the basis of the best information you have at that time.

Leadership is like that: you make a decision on the basis of the best information you have at that time. But when circumstances change, you may need to rethink and revise your strategy to meet the new conditions without being too proud or stoic to do so.

HOW TO TAKE COMMAND

Take Command begins with accepting that differences of opinion are usually ideological rather than personal. However, there is ample research to support that societal perceptions and expectations of women in command are different from those for men in equivalent roles and that women are often judged more harshly. Additionally, in nations where White male leaders are the societal norm (especially in America, where I live and work), the perceptions and expectations for women of color are different than those for White women. For example, women of color experience closer scrutiny of their credentials, as a whole are paid less than others in comparable positions, must demonstrate greater competency on social issues, and are subject to the negative stereotypes associated with being a woman in addition to those that are attributed to their race/ethnicity.[21]

Leadership expectations for both men and women these days are quite different from those that were the norm a generation or so ago. A generation ago, the typical leader was male, stern, authoritative, and reserved; emotion was equated with weakness, and sharing too much about one's personal life was taboo. Any woman who aspired to leadership needed to demonstrate these characteristics as well. These days, however, any leader, whether male or female, who wants to appeal to a broad cross-section of the population or workforce and inspire their loyalty is encouraged to make a genuine effort to show their empathetic, human side. If you aspire to influence, you cannot afford to ignore societal perceptions and expectations regarding your personal style and approach to Take Command. Even though societal stereotypes and perceptions are slowly changing, I question

---

21   While it is beyond the scope of this chapter to address the challenges associated with the intersection of race and gender, I have included a list of resources you can find at http://www.TakeSixHabits.com/.

whether they will ever completely disappear, as every generation will set expectations born of their experience, and you certainly cannot disregard those expectations on your path to leadership. At the same time, there are some perennial leadership qualities that instill confidence and respect, even when people may disagree with you.

People want to know that the person they are following is prepared for the command they have undertaken; that's why it is important to be adept at communicating your accomplishments (i.e., habit 3: Take Credit) as well as owning your decision when you put it forward. Remember Clare, the indecisive CEO? Clare's problem wasn't so much the decisions themselves, but the fact that it always sounded as though she lacked clear opinions of her own and was just parroting her predecessor's approach regarding the right course of action. Her behavior in meetings reinforced this impression. As important as it is to listen carefully to conflicting points of view, look at the situation from all sides, and even be open to allow new information to change your perspective, there comes a time when leaders need to make a decision based on the best information that they have available at hand that is consistent with their bigger vision. That's a leader's responsibility. You must be decisive and lead.

When you are soliciting opposing opinions, here are some questions that you can use to draw people out and get a 360-degree view:

- How would we … ?
- How might we … ?
- How would we respond if … ?
- How are we doing on … ?
- What would happen (or not happen) if we … ?
- What have I overlooked about … ?

- What is the other side of ... ?

- What alternatives could we consider ... ?

- What am I missing or not seeing ... ?

- What is wrong with this approach ... ?

- What has prevented us from ... ?

- Whom else should I consult or ask for input ... ?

These questions, and others like them, tend to draw out contrasting opinions and encourage exploration of issues from other angles and perspectives. As a lawyer, I was trained to ask "how" questions to open up possibilities. "What" questions follow naturally from "how" questions when the time comes to elaborate on strategy and develop a practical course of action. "Why" questions can prove least useful because they tend to lead to justification and blame. However, "why" questions are entirely appropriate and necessary for purposes of mitigating risk, especially ways to prevent recurrence of negative outcomes.

Depending on the situation, these questions might be framed around your thinking, your actions, or other people's responses. It's important to use "possibility" words, like *might* and *would*, rather than "necessity" words like *should*, *must*, and *need* during these discussions.

After the discussions are over (or after the time allotted for discussion is exhausted), it's time for you to express your position clearly and concisely. The most effective leaders will express this decision and acknowledge the other options that have not been chosen as well as the challenges that your chosen course presents. In the haste to communicate a decision and move on, I am often guilty of failing to heed this advice, and it is something that I am continually seeking to improve. No leader is perfect, but we should all strive to learn and grow.

RELINQUISHING COMMAND

No corporate leadership role lasts forever, and how you behave when you turn over command is critical for the future of your organization. Clare, whose failure I mentioned earlier, was responsible for not truly taking command of the organization when she was appointed as CEO, but her predecessor was also guilty of not stepping aside when his time was over. As far as we could see, he was quite happy to tell Clare what she should do rather than challenge her to own the situation and take control in her way.

I have been extremely grateful to Fred Krebs, my predecessor at ACC, for being so gracious with his support and generous with his advice when I requested it, but especially for his recognition that it was my turn to put a stamp on the role and lead the organization. Perhaps this is easier when you leave after a successful run as a leader, or when you leave to step into another leadership role. When I left MCCA, I was acutely aware of the importance of leaving my successor room to shine, and it helped that I was extremely busy learning the ropes at ACC. While I remain a strong supporter of the important work MCCA is doing today under the capable leadership of Jean Lee to advance diversity, when we catch up over lunch, we are sharing ideas, triumphs, challenges, and solutions as equals and as owners of our own programs. Jean's energy, enthusiasm, and dedication to MCCA's mission is exactly what the organization needs, and I am proud to see her taking up the mantle of leadership on an issue that is so critically important to the legal profession and the future of countless diverse lawyers.

TAKE COMMAND OF YOUR LIFE

Maybe you don't currently aspire to be the person who heads an organization, community, or nation, or even be the person at the front of the room, and that is fine if that is your choice. However, there is another choice that we all have to face: whether to be passive or active when it comes to controlling our own lives.

Originally, there were only five habits that I viewed as critical: Take Stock, Take Risk, Take Credit, Take a Hand, and Take a Stand. To be honest, thanks to my mother's teaching that being popular and pleasing others wasn't the most important thing, I thought that Take Command was only relevant for public figures. Over the years of mentoring hundreds of professionals, I realized that a large number of adults were still living the lives that parents or other authority figures had designed for them, but it wasn't until December 2019 that I appreciated the full extent of the danger this abdication presents. During the Democratic presidential primaries on national television and live-streamed the world over, five of the candidates running for the office of president of the United States were invited to speak to their own abilities and achievements and offer either an apology or a gift to their peers. The three men each eloquently described their accomplishments and offered a gift; the two women, both US senators with many years of service behind them, asked forgiveness for their passionate engagement and vocal championship of causes they had supported. I was so crushed and disappointed that I felt angry. How could anyone seeking the US presidency apologize for doing what a leader must do: chart a

> **There is another choice that we all have to face: whether to be passive or active when it comes to controlling our own lives.**

course and passionately advocate so that others are inspired to follow!

When we move outside the political arena, it's not only women who hesitate to Take Command of their own lives. Many grown men and women are still following the paths laid out for them by other well-meaning people and apologizing for who they are. They may have gone into medicine, finance, law, or engineering because these are prestigious careers and chose to suppress other interests, gifts, and abilities that might have had a stronger appeal or been better aligned with their gifts and personalities. The bravest people I know have had the courage to reverse course and forge a brand-new path that is uniquely their own, and they offer real-life examples of the impact of these six habits. So I have three quick reflections to wind up this chapter on Take Command:

> **You only have one life to live—do not waste it apologizing for who you are and what you have or have not done.**

1. You only have one life to live—make sure you take full responsibility for its direction and Take Command of your destiny.

2. You only have one life to live—do not try to relive your life through your children, students, or anyone else. Command your life, not theirs.

3. You only have one life to live—do not waste it apologizing for who you are and what you have or have not done. Learn from your mistakes, and don't let your regrets or fears stop you from focusing on being the best **you** that you can be in this present moment and beyond.

As you Take Command of your own life and follow the path that unwinds in front of you, like any leader, you need to listen to other people with contrary opinions, evaluate their positions, and then choose the path that best expresses your own vision to make a difference in the world. It is you who will be held accountable.

Now that we have examined in detail the six habits that will enable you to own your destiny, overcome challenges, and unlock opportunities, let's look at where this could take you and what you need to do now.

IN CHAPTER 7 YOU LEARNED:

- Take Command is about personal accountability and responsibility for what you stand for and will achieve, more than what you oppose or won't do.
- Inviting discussion and actively seeking alternate viewpoints is important and encouraged, but ultimately taking command will mean making decisions, being responsible for follow-through, and accepting accountability for the results. While communication, consensus building, and inclusion are important, often your decision will not make everyone happy. As a leader, you need to be OK with that.
- Apologizing for being passionate about your vision and seeking agreement at all costs may erode confidence in a leader's ability, notwithstanding her achievements.
- Men may need to make a concerted effort to project empathy and their "human side" so that they appear more authentic and relatable to wider audiences.

- Delay and indecision create doubt and can ultimately undermine leadership.
- If your goal is popularity, then taking command is likely not for you. All leaders have to make tough calls, and that comes with the job.

TAKE SIX

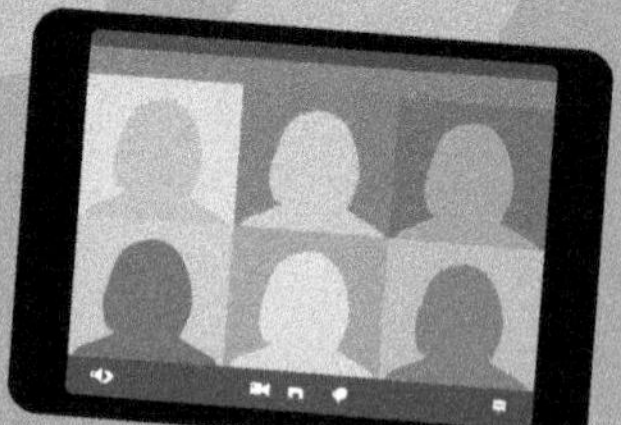

CHAPTER EIGHT

GO SOAR
AND MAKE
AN IMPACT

Every great dream begins with a dreamer. Always remember,
you have within you the strength, the patience, and the
passion to reach for the stars to change the world.

—HARRIET TUBMAN

Some years ago, I was on vacation with my sister and two longtime friends, and we were talking about the important role artistic expression and theatrical experience play in developing confidence, passion, multicultural understanding, empathy, and communication skills, especially in young people. All four of us are actively engaged in mentoring and passionately committed to helping others express their talents and fulfill their dreams in their own way. In fact, we have each done that ourselves as we have pursued completely different pathways in different fields.

A chance remark about the lack of focus on these things in current education systems, especially those aimed at helping disadvantaged and minority children, led to an impassioned debate about the most effective paths to change the world and give more people a voice. At the end of that holiday, my sister and I continued to talk, and not long after returning to our homes, we had sketched out a plan for a nonprofit that would run sponsored summer programs for disadvantaged youth (disadvantaged culturally, economically, or educationally). These programs would focus on unleashing their creative talent, exploring means and consequences of self-expression, and equipping them with the confidence to speak up for their goals and ideals. Our vision was for a truly global foundation with programs that could be implemented anywhere in the world.

When we shared this idea with others, we sometimes got the response, "But aren't there already programs that do this kind of thing, as well as drama classes at school?" There is some justification for this question, but neither my sister nor I are satisfied with waiting for others to create change. We both look at what **we** can do to make a difference ourselves, and we have seen firsthand the power of these programs to build critical skills of collaboration, communication, and self-confidence as well as the gaps in current opportunities and offerings. Historically, the arts have often spearheaded social understanding, and we want the Global Community Arts Foundation that we formed in fulfillment of our dream to be part of that enabling across cultures in our own time.

As I look around at societies throughout the world, we believe that there are few things more important than equipping young people with the skills to express who they are and communicate what they believe as well as pursue their dreams.

HOW THIS BOOK CAME TO BE WRITTEN

When the idea of writing a book was first suggested to me, I said to myself, "Who am I to write a book? I haven't done anything sensational, I am not a household name, and I am very far from done with my life and ambitions." However, the suggestion stayed in my mind, and it was reinforced when my mentees and people who heard me speak wished they had my ideas written down so they could refer to them easily. As I thought about the contribution I want to make to the world, the unconquered horizons I would like to scale, and the processes I would use to achieve those goals, I realized that I had something valuable to contribute to a wider audience and that these essential habits play just as important a role in my career today as they did when I was starting out with only a murky view of what it would take to achieve my goals.

Writing this book has helped me Take Stock of where I am and think about my next steps in my goal to leave this world a kinder and better place than when I entered it. My work is far from over, and the challenges of the global pandemic and societal tensions have highlighted the importance of having a vision for growth and cohesion. I'm also building the relationships, credibility, and experience needed to achieve my goal of sitting on the board of directors of a public company and fulfilling the dream of my eight-year-old self who has always been curious and interested in how businesses run.

Are those dreams and the dream of bridging societal divides to stamp out injustices beyond my reach? We don't always get what we want, no matter how hard we work, but it's only when we give up on our dreams and stop moving toward them that we're guaranteed to miss the mark.

WHAT ABOUT YOU?

I don't believe that anyone comes into this world with the intention to merely make sure they are fed, clothed, and sheltered until they can finally die in peace. If you have read to this point, I am confident that you have bigger goals than that.

- What is your big goal for your life?
- In what area would you like to make an impact and help others?
- What are you going to do to make it a reality?

I've noticed that people often graduate with high aspirations and expectations, but by their late twenties or early thirties, the realities of the marketplace, the realization that there are many people just as diligent and talented as they are, and the tolls that years of unrelenting study and work have taken on their brain and body leave them exhausted and uninspired. There's a simple reason for this lapse: you cannot be, do, and have everything that you want if you do not take care of your body, mind, and soul. That means staying hydrated, taking time every single day to breathe deeply so carbon dioxide doesn't build up in your lungs, eat well to fuel your body and brain, move regularly to strengthen and stretch your muscles, read and learn to keep your mind fresh and overflowing with ideas, and make sure you get sufficient sleep. It also means taking time off for proper vacations and liberally sprinkling your weeks with time for family, friends, and hobbies. That is basic self-care, and it does underlie everything else.

While I do not profess to following my own good advice 100 percent of the time, one practice that has always helped me feel grounded and recommitted is making time for gratitude. Parkinson's Law tells us that work expands to fill the time available; the mental corollary of this law is that what we focus on expands and fills our attention. The more you focus on things you are grateful for, the happier and more productive you will be. There are some days that my schedule is overflowing, and the demands of work and life seem almost impossible. Those are the days when I make it a priority to stop, take a deep breath, and focus on the things I am grateful for, even though they fuel my crazy-busy professional and personal schedule.

> **Your "gratitude attitude" really does help you focus on why all these things are your responsibilities in the first place, and it generates the positive energy you need to do them with excellence.**

Your "gratitude attitude" really does help you focus on why all these things are your responsibilities in the first place, and it generates the positive energy you need to do them with excellence.

PEOPLE GROW AND CHANGE

Gratitude and self-care are all very well, but what if you realize in your thirties, forties, or fifties, or even later, that the work that you used to enjoy is now simply a habit, and you want to change direction or shift your emphasis?

Just because you start on one trajectory doesn't mean that you can't change when opportunity knocks or dissatisfaction takes hold.

Remember my godmother, Jeanette, who was not afraid to start college much later in life? It's never too late to make a change or to find success doing something entirely different.

Emmy Award–winning journalist, author, and cohost of ABC's *The View* (the number one–ranked daytime television show in the United States) Sunny Hostin exemplifies a woman who did not allow self-doubt or challenges along the way to deter her from pursuing her dreams. Although Sunny's first legal stint was as a federal prosecutor specializing in child sex crimes, I met her while I was heading MCCA and she was a leading global investigator of business fraud. We were sorors (AKA) and shared the desire to make a difference as outspoken advocates for diversity in the legal profession. The folks in the MCCA network cheered Sunny on and took pride seeing someone we knew make a big transition to television and journalism. Her journey started with the opportunity to be a part-time commentator for Court TV, and she thought, "Why not? It might be fun."

It **was** fun for Sunny, and she proved good at it. When she was offered additional roles, she decided that she wanted to commit fully to TV journalism, sharing her legal expertise on a global stage, and exploring new opportunities. She now costars on a top-ranked television program with millions of fans.

Sunny was already successful when she shifted careers, but you cannot say the same about Colonel Sanders, who was in his forties when he started serving chicken dishes and other meals at a Shell service station in Kentucky, and sixty-two when he opened his first KFC franchise restaurant in 1952. He didn't start out as a cook or restaurateur, though. His previous career included a stint in the US Army, various railroad jobs, legal practice, establishing a ferry boat company, and a career in sales as he strove to support his family through the

Great Depression and beyond. He never saw his age as a barrier to trying something new in his search for a satisfying and profitable career that would support his family and provide employment for others.

One of my personal heroes is Nelson Mandela. Born in South Africa to the Thembu royal family, Mandela had a privileged upbringing and became a lawyer. He could have chosen to enjoy his personal comforts, but he chose to fight for the rights of his own people, who did not all share his societal stature. As a result of being a freedom fighter against a deeply rooted and unjust system of apartheid, Mandela spent twenty-seven years in one of the harshest prisons in South Africa, eventually released and elected president of his country at the age of seventy-five. From privilege to prison to president, perhaps his greatest legacy of transition was his voluntary relinquishment of power as he refused to serve a second term as president and took on the mantle of elder statesman and champion of democracy and social justice, leaving a legacy felt the world over.

WHERE ARE YOU NOW?

I don't know exactly where you are in your career as you are reading this book. Maybe you are

- at college trying to decide what to do next ...
- already on the path to your goals and looking for advice and encouragement ...
- looking for the next step in your established career ...
- looking for a career change, whether voluntary or involuntary ...
- retired and wondering what to do now ...

I do know that if you've read this far, you're serious about making the next stage of your life even more meaningful and satisfying than anything that has gone before.

This book is designed to be used, not simply read—so here is your homework ...

STEP ONE: TAKE STOCK NOW!

Either sit down right now, or schedule a time this week in your calendar for this exercise.

- Write down where you have come from, where you are now, and where you want to go. If your goal isn't yet fixed, that's fine. You can change it later (I have done so many times), but identify the highest goal you can think of at this moment.

- Identify and write down any gaps that you need to fill in your education, experience, network, skills, et cetera. Create an action timeline.

- What have you already accomplished or contributed? If you haven't done this before, it can help to think back in three-month chunks of time, and try to identify three or four achievements or contributions for each period. You'll use these to Take Credit, and you'll track them as part of taking stock.

- From now on, make tracking your achievements, contributions, and value a weekly priority.

You are where you are today because of the choices you have made consciously or unconsciously and the work you did or did not do. Where you go from here is equally your choice, but this time, you can consciously make choices that align with your goals and your gifts and make yourself unstoppable.

STEP TWO: TAKE RISK

Comfort is the enemy of growth and also of your goals. You don't need to spend every moment at full stretch in the risk department, and it is always helpful to have at least one area of your life that is in a familiar routine, but when you make comfort an ongoing commitment, you are at risk of stagnation.

- Spend time making a list of the top five things that make you fearful or worried about making a change. Now, what would you do if those fears or worries did not exist?

- What next steps do you have on your horizon for your personal and professional goals?

- Is there a decision that you have been postponing or avoiding because it involves risk?

- If you have already achieved everything you've dreamed of, then it is time to set your sights on something bigger so you don't become too comfortable or complacent.

STEP THREE: TAKE CREDIT

In taking credit, you have developed the habit of tracking your accomplishments and contributions. By sharing them, you increase the potential for opportunities to come your way because you've shown you are capable and talented. If you are just starting to think in these terms, it's important to go back as far as you can remember so that you have plenty of data to back up your credibility and help others recognize the value you bring to the table.

- Now that you are making weekly—or, at minimum, monthly—notes of your contributions and accomplishments in specific projects, notice how your work and contributions relate to larger initiatives of your organization or group. Your objective is to identify ways to bring them into conversations with peers and superiors without sounding like bragging.

- Think about how your accomplishments and projects that support departmental initiatives also contribute to wider company goals.

- Once you understand how what you contribute fits and feeds into a larger organizational context, you are ready to revamp how you speak about your contributions and achievements.

- Focus on how your work contributes to achieving something bigger rather than listing completed tasks.

- Practice (role-playing is a great tool for this exercise) talking naturally about your contribution in the light of company or project goals. Tell that nagging voice in your head that what you are doing is **taking ownership** of your work and **sharing** with people who ought and need to know.

Remember these three things:

1. If you do not share your accomplishments and contributions, you cannot expect that anyone will know about them.

2. Their knowledge of your accomplishments increases the likelihood of your consideration for other opportunities.

3. The simple act of reviewing and considering these things regularly means that they are likely to be top of mind and will therefore naturally come out in your conversations as statements of fact or sharing things that others should know about.

STEP FOUR: TAKE A HAND

There is no such thing as a "self-made man," no matter how attractive this idea seems to be. We are all standing on the shoulders of those who have gone before us and paved the way, and it seems to me that being willing to acknowledge our interdependence is an important characteristic for success.

- The twin questions—"Whom am I helping?" and "Who is helping me?"—are potent indicators of both present and future achievement. Your answers to them will tell you a great deal about the kind of person you are now and the kind of person you will be in the future.

- What are you going to do in response to your answers to those questions about who you are helping, especially if your answer to either is coming up short?

- Who can help you take the next step in your career? Identify whether you need advice, recommendations, mentors, opportunities, or something else, and determine what needs to happen so that you are in a position to ask for that thing.

- Whom can you help, and how can you do so? It's never too soon to think about giving a hand to others, even if it's just a question of sharing your mistakes and thoughts as well as the lessons you have learned so far.

- Whether your approach is to turn to mentors, seek advisors, get a coach, use a buddy system, or turn to a teacher, there are multiple opportunities to reach for help.

Where you conclude that you are not really doing a good job asking for help or helping others, my advice is to start with helping others first. It may sound counterintuitive, and you may be tempted to focus first on yourself and what you need or want from others. I believe that is the wrong approach because when you start by extending yourself in service of others, you will gain confidence, Take Stock of all you have to share (i.e., two habits strengthened), and be better prepared to ask for, and utilize, the help you will seek and receive from others as you commit to Take a Hand.

STEP FIVE: TAKE A STAND

Your willingness to stand up for the values you hold, the vision you follow, and the rights of other human beings creates trust. When those around you know that you will firmly uphold what you believe and your actions match your stated values, you will earn their respect, and people will be more inclined to trust your judgment and character, even when they may disagree with your decisions.

- What cause do you believe in so firmly that you would be willing to risk anything and pay any price to stand up for it? How are you contributing to that cause?

- Have you observed behavior and attitudes that belittle or discount others? Think about what you could do or say to stand up against it next time you hear or see it.

- Is there some behavior or attitude that others display toward you that you have been putting up with? How would you Take a Stand and seek change, especially if you knew that you would not be the only person to benefit?

STEP SIX: TAKE COMMAND

Whether it is institutional leadership (command of a nation or company), or situational leadership, leaders primarily stand for something: values, a course of action, project outcomes, viewpoints, et cetera, and they do what it takes to advance their cause. However, I will qualify this by underscoring that while good leaders are willing to do whatever it takes to get the job done, they do not compromise ethically, violate societal norms of civility, bully, lie, or disrespect others in the process.

When you are the person in command, it is your responsibility to take ownership of the course of action. But first ...

- In an emergency, prompt, purposeful action is critical. If there's no time for discourse and discussion, then just go ahead and do what needs to be done using your best judgment.

- Whenever possible, you should actively solicit objections and alternative points of view from those around you. There is rarely only one right course of action, and it's important to consider alternatives and make sure that those around you feel heard.

- Once you have decided the direction you will take, do not waste time trying to convince 100 percent of the people to accept your way of thinking; universal agreement or approval may not be possible, and you will have to be comfortable with that. The time for seeking consensus is before the decision is made, not afterward. Getting buy-in from stakeholders is important for effective execution, but when universal buy-in isn't possible, most reasonable people will follow a plan of action that is clearly and effectively communicated to acknowledge contrary views, share transparency of process, and objectively outline the next steps.

- Lastly, leadership means stepping up to fill a void that needs to be addressed for common good. Your impact may be felt in ways large or small—Take Command of a situation, if only to uplift another's spirit, as that's leadership too.

SMALL STEPS CAN HAVE BIG OUTCOMES

In 1960, six-year-old Ruby Bridges was escorted to her new school in New Orleans by US Deputy Marshals. She was the first Black child to attend an all-White school in New Orleans, and that year she was the only child in her class. The parents of three other Black children who had been accepted were persuaded to send their children elsewhere, and White parents would not send their children there because of Ruby's presence.

The law said one thing; social opinion said another. At one point, the crowds who turned up to protest her attendance brought a small coffin with a Black doll inside and displayed it outside the gate. Ruby used to have nightmares about that box. Her parents also suffered. Grocery stores refused to serve her mother, and her father lost his job as a consequence of their stand. The following year when Ruby started second grade, the incoming first-grade class had eight Black students. Her parents made a courageous decision that would impact their whole community, and Ruby (with their love and support) took a stand.

If Ruby's parents had not stood up for their rights ... if Ruby had not endured the persecution and singularity ... if the school had not complied with the law (however reluctantly) ... if Ruby's teacher had not broken rank with the others who refused to instruct a Black child ... things might be very different today. A picture of little Ruby hangs in my office over my shoulder, and when I feel overwhelmed or doubtful, looking at her determined little face gives me a boost to forge on. Never underestimate the impact you can have. We are each capable of taking command, whether it takes the form of institutional, situational, or personal leadership. So before you dismiss your dreams or trim them down to "manageable size," think of the impact one six-year-old girl had on an entire country, and remember that each person has that same power to change the course of history ... including you.

TAKE SIX

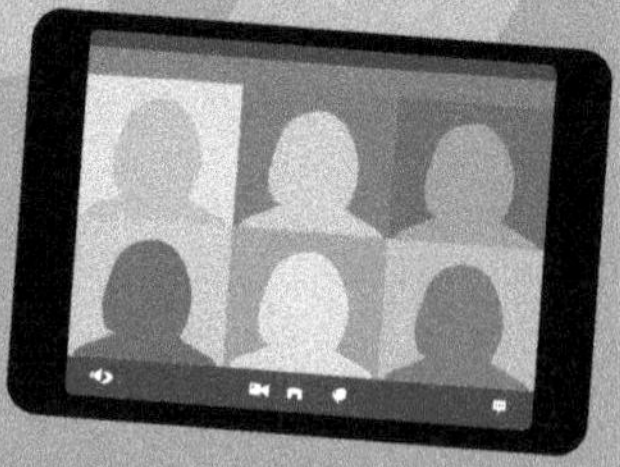

CONCLUSION

Our destiny is not written for us; it's written by us.

—BARACK OBAMA

THE DIFFERENCE "TAKE SIX" MAKES

On a sunny day in May, more years ago than seems possible, I graduated from the University of Maryland Law School along with my cohort. We were all good students with high hopes and aspirations—intelligent, motivated, diligent, ambitious. In the long run, that was not always enough.

I've told many of my own stories throughout this book and how passionate I am about practicing and sharing these six habits, and the following story illustrates why it's so important. I'll tell you about a dear friend whom I will call Sarah, recognizing that names and some details have been changed to protect her identity. Sarah and I were friends throughout law school, and we often studied together; we were even roommates for a few years. She was a smart student, and her grades in some subjects were higher than mine. After graduation she went into the Department of the Public Prosecutor, and her managers anticipated a shining career in litigation, given her quick wit and persuasive oratory skill. Around the time that I was thinking of leaving Sunoco and diligently taking stock of my options, Sarah was also thinking about what she wanted to do, because she was "tired of prosecuting ordinary people and wanted something more challenging."

Sarah was invited to join a small firm that represented high-profile sports and entertainment personalities with designs on expanding to attract more clients like that. For Sarah, this was a dream job that represented novelty, fame, and challenge, so she leaped at the opportunity. Within a few weeks of hearing about this opportunity for the first time, she took a risk and abandoned her secure job and prospects of advancement (burning many relationships, including our friendship, in the process) to start her role in this new field. It wasn't until after she started there that she discovered that they only had one client of the type she was looking for, and that relationship was on somewhat rocky ground. Sarah had simply never asked the right questions and only heard what she wanted to hear, even as many people tried to counsel her to be cautious.

It wasn't long before Sarah was arguing with her new boss and contesting his way of doing things, and a short time later, she had no choice but to leave the firm. As our conversations shifted from her hopes and dreams, to her struggles, and then to her humiliation at losing her job, I tried to help her Take Stock, evaluate, and mitigate the risks of her decision and restart her career, but she wasn't really willing to listen to my advice. Unfortunately, since I was in the corporate world (too humdrum and boring for her), I didn't have many connections in private practice at the time. In any case, to be honest, Sarah didn't ask advice or Take a Hand easily. She had always been proud of her ability to work things out herself and not depend on others, and now she was angry and aggrieved at the unfairness of it all. She wouldn't even consider asking her previous employer for opportunities or recommendations to other departments, and she had never been very good at tracking her achievements so that other people could see her contribution: in her eyes, if someone couldn't see and appreciate her qualities without prompting, then that was their problem, not hers.

I didn't recognize it at the time, but one of Sarah's weaknesses was an inability to constructively deal with conflict or even disagreement. At the first sign of tension, she would withdraw and resort to passive aggression. It made her seem an easygoing, fun person, but in reality, she was a difficult coworker because she would ignore or downplay problems instead of admitting her shortcomings and asking questions before those problems were too big to be overlooked any longer.

Like many high-potential people, she thought that being tough, smart, and driven could take her anywhere ... but ultimately those strengths became her downfall because they weren't linked with these six habits.

Despite her mistakes, it wouldn't have been too late for Sarah to Take Stock of her options and make a plan that could have placed her in the position she wanted: representing sports and entertainment figures. It wasn't her goal that was the problem, but her methodology, her pride, and her tendency to disregard others who cared enough to say what she had difficulty hearing. Like many high-potential people, she thought that being tough, smart, and driven could take her anywhere ... but ultimately those strengths became her downfall because they weren't linked with these six habits.

WHAT IS THE DIFFERENCE?

It really does boil down to the consistent practice of these six essential tried-and-tested habits. If you Take Stock and close the gaps but don't want to Take a Risk, you will become stagnant, despite being prepared. If you Take Risk without a solid plan, you may be prone to fail, especially if you are too proud or arrogant to ask for and Take a Hand. If you learn to Take Credit, you will be well equipped to stand up for yourself when someone attempts to minimize your contributions or steal credit for your hard work. And the opportunity to lead or Take Command will hopefully come your way as the first five habits become second nature for you and lead you to the sixth. Sarah's outcomes could have been very different, and who knows where she could have been today if she had made different choices, been more open to constructive feedback, and been disciplined enough to adopt these essential six habits?

You do not need to wait for permission from anyone to move forward.

If you have aspirations in any field or role and want to shape your own destiny and open up more opportunities, you have already seen how you can use these essential habits:

- Take Stock

- Take Risk

- Take Credit

- Take a Hand

- Take a Stand

- Take Command

You do not need to wait for permission from anyone to move forward, nor do you need to wish that you had been born in a different country, era, or parentage. All you need to do is to take hold of this moment that you have been given to look within and see your potential, decide what you actually want, and then adopt these six habits to chart a way to make it happen.

May these six habits provide the strong base that you need to build firm foundations, pursue ever-growing dreams, achieve your goals, and become a leader and role model that others will be inspired to follow.

The Beginning.

TAKE SIX

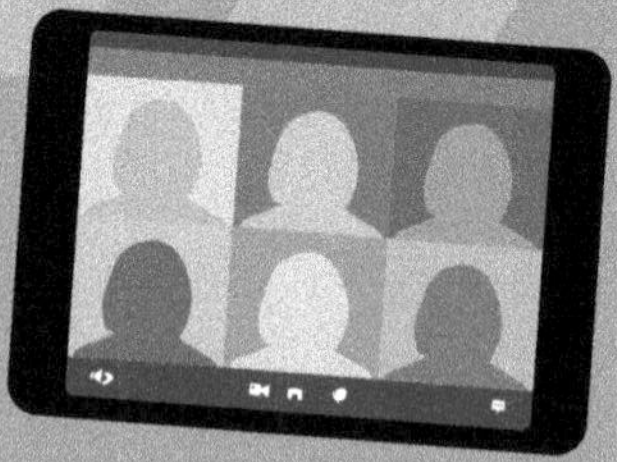

ACKNOWLEDGMENTS

This book would not have been possible without Debra Hilton. Debra is the talented writer who helped me bring my stories and thoughts to you in a way that reflects the intersection of my own unique voice and her literary ability. Debra, you are hardly a "ghostwriter," as your talent is very real, seen, and deeply appreciated. I am so grateful for our weekly Zoom meetings over the span of more than six months—you in Melbourne, me in Maryland, both of us living through a pandemic, just trying to stay healthy, socially distant, and sane. Thank you!

When I started on this journey to write a book, I had no idea how much work it would entail and how many people it would involve. The idea of a book came from the many students and young lawyers whom I met at conferences, through law firms, bar associations, or my teaching who asked me how I plotted my path from law school to my present position. Through this year of lockdowns and political turmoil, I've been grateful for the purpose this book has given to my leisure hours, so I'd like to acknowledge you all and thank you for inspiring me to begin this project.

Chapter 5 of this book focuses on taking a hand, and in it I point out that when you extend a hand to another person, you have a wonderful opportunity to reflect on your own learnings. I've discovered that writing a book that is designed to help people whom I may never meet in person magnifies that process. As I selected the stories and exercises to amplify and illustrate each of these habits, I realized how much I owe to my many mentors, colleagues, students, and models throughout my career. Some of you are credited in this book; others are unnamed, but your words and ways have taught me valuable lessons, and I wouldn't be where I am today without you. Thank you!

The team at Advantage|ForbesBooks has been an incredible resource, guiding me through the complicated process of writing, editing, publishing, and marketing my book. Thank you to Conor for introducing me to Advantage|ForbesBooks, Rachel for coordinating the team and the process, Kristin for suggesting the best-ever writing partner (Debra), Josh for your edits and helpful comments, David for working with me to design an awesome and engaging cover, Rusty for his marketing guidance and expertise on connecting with my audience, and Melani for helping with the development and presentation of content beyond the book to further reach my audience. Cheers to what we've achieved together!

Finally, I'd like to thank my late mom and dad, who taught me by word and example the habits in this book and encouraged me to believe in myself, to work hard, and never to let anyone crush my dreams, *and* my family, friends, and colleagues who encouraged and supported me throughout this project. Whenever I felt discouraged and concerned that it was too hard, too intense, or too revealing, you reminded me that nothing worthwhile happens without risk. Along with the unconditional love of my sixteen-year-old adorable toy poodle, Buster, you make my journey so rewarding!

CPSIA information can be obtained
at www.ICGtesting.com
Printed in the USA
BVHW090724010522
635227BV00005B/10/J